D0103858

In Pursuit

of

Purpose

by Myles Munroe

© Copyright 1992 — Myles Munroe

All rights reserved. This book is protected under the copyright laws of the United States of America. This book may not be copied or reprinted for commercial gain or profit. The use of short quotations or occasional page copying for personal or group study is permitted and encouraged. Permission will be granted upon request. Unless otherwise identified, Scripture quotations are from the New International Version of the Bible. Quotations from the King James Version have been denoted (KJV), from the New King James Version as (NKJV), from the Easy-to-Read Version as (ETRV), and from the Good News Today's English Version as (GN). All emphasis within quotations is the author's addition.

Take note that the name satan and related names are not capitalized. We choose not to acknowledge him, even to the point of violating grammatical rules.

Destiny Image® Publishers, Inc.
P.O. Box 310
Shippensburg, PA 17257-0310

"Speaking to the Purposes of God for This
Generation and for the Generations to Come"

Bahamas Faith Ministry
P.O. Box N9583
Nassau, Bahamas

ISBN 1-56043-103-2

For Worldwide Distribution
Printed in the U.S.A.

Twenty-seventh Printing: 2003   Twenty-eighth Printing: 2004

This book and all other Destiny Image, Revival Press,
MercyPlace, Fresh Bread, Destiny Image Fiction,
and Treasure House books are available
at Christian bookstores and distributors worldwide.

For a U.S. bookstore nearest you, call **1-800-722-6774**.
For more information on foreign distributors,
call **717-532-3040**.
Or reach us on the Internet: **www.destinyimage.com**

Contents

Dedication
Acknowledgments
Foreword
Preface
Introduction

Dedication

To the human heart.

To every individual given birth by destiny.

To the one who finds life empty, aimless and busy,
but not effective.

To you, the reader, for whom I desire a purposeful
life characterized by effectiveness, efficiency and
fulfillment.

To all who are oppressed by the ignorance of others.

To every generation that seeks meaning and a reason
for living.

To everyone who is seeking for himself.

Acknowledgments

We are a sum total of what we have learned from all who have taught us, both great and small. I am grateful for the inspiration and wisdom of men and women of God and for the transgenerational sources and roots of wisdom they have left me.

I am also grateful for the many members, friends and colleagues at Bahamas Faith Ministries International whose faithfulness, prayers and patience inspire me to continue to fulfill my purpose and potential.

For the development and production of this book itself, I feel a deep sense of gratitude to:

—my precious wife, Ruth, and our children, Charisa and Chairo (Myles Jr.), for their patience and support during my travels outside the home. You make it easier to fulfill God's will for my life.

—my father and mother, Matt and Louise Munroe, for their devotion to the Lord and to their children, and for their constant demonstration of love that inspired me to pursue the maximization of my potential.

—my dear friend and brother-in-law, Richard Pinder, whose commitment to the work and the vision makes this project possible.

—Kathy Miller, my gifted and diligent editor and advisor, who shepherded the book from its early formless stage to its present form, and Marsha Blessing of Destiny Image, who patiently pursued me to keep to the schedule and meet the deadlines.

—the best friends in the ministry I can ever have—Turnel Nelson, Bertril Baird, Peter Morgan, John Smith, Kingsley Fletcher, Fuschia Pickett, Ezekiel Guti, Jerry Horner, Mensa Otabil, Cecil Lamb and Ben Kinchlow—for exposing my potential.

Foreword

"Who am I?" "Why am I here?" These questions are among the oldest put forth by honest men and women who are seeking answers to the age-old question, "What is life about?"

It is an unfortunate truth that many people live with a quiet desperation and some die plagued by the vague uneasiness that somehow they have "missed it." Others wander aimlessly—a few purposefully—attempting to solve the puzzle posed by life.

Many Christians have proclaimed that salvation is the "be all and end all" of life here. Salvation is certainly the single most important element in time and eternity, but there are many "truly saved" Christians who feel unfulfilled even as they agonize, fast and pray in an attempt to salve the nagging sense that there is something more to life. Yes, they know Jesus. Yes, many have been filled with the Holy Spirit. Still, the great majority wonder, "What lies beyond salvation and the baptism of the Spirit?"

In Pursuit of Purpose goes a long way toward answering these questions. No single book except the Bible can answer all your questions, but drawing from the wellspring of divine revelation, life experience and intelligent scholarship, Dr. Myles Munroe has fashioned a compass that can focus you on the path toward fulfillment, while providing the answer to the all-encompassing question, "Why am I here?"

You have not picked up this book by accident. You haven't wandered here aimlessly. There is method to this journey and a solution may be at hand. Perhaps, you will find in these pages what you have been seeking for years—purpose.

Ben Kinchlow
The 700 Club
Virginia Beach, VA

Preface

The greatest tragedy in life is not death, but life without a reason. It is dangerous to be alive and not know why you were given life. One of the most frustrating experiences is to have time but not know why.

From the beginning of man's history as we know it, mankind has been grappling with the age-old questions: Why am I here? What is the reason for my existence? What is the meaning of my life? Is there a reason for the universe, the creation and man? These questions are universal. They lurk deep within the secret chambers of every human being on earth regardless of their race, color, ethnic heritage, socioeconomic status or nationality. Philosophers such as Plato, Aristotle, Socrates and others throughout the ages have attempted to explore these seemingly illusive questions. For the most part, their efforts have ended in more questions than answers.

The deepest craving of the human spirit is to find a sense of significance and relevance. The search for relevance in life is the ultimate pursuit of man. Conscious or unconscious, admitted or unadmitted, this internal passion is what motivates and drives every human being, either directly or indirectly. It directs his decisions, controls his behavior and dictates his responses to his environment.

This need for significance is the cause of great tragedies. Many suicides and attempted suicides owe their manifestation to this compelling need. Many mass murderers and serial killers confess the relationship of their antisocial behavior to their need to feel important or to experience a sense of self-worth.

This passion for relevance and a sense of significance makes one race or ethnic group elevate itself above another. It also gives birth to prejudice and causes the fabrication of erroneous perceptions that result in grave injustices and the conception of abominable dreams and inhuman behavior. It also gives birth to tyrants and dictators who easily sacrifice the sacredness of human life and dignity for a temporary sense of significance.

This desperate desire to feel important and relevant to one's existence also causes the sacrifice of common sense, good judgment, moral standards and basic human values. Many individuals have sacrificed excellent reputations and years of character-building life styles for the sake of advancement to a desired position, or a place of recognition and fame in their society or workplace, so they could feel important and worthwhile.

This passion for a sense of significance and meaning in life is also the fuel for most capitalist and progressive economies. There are millions of individuals who sacrifice their families, friends and convictions in the attempt to gain a sense of significance. Accumulating status symbols and material possessions, they seek a position of importance and meaning.

In essence, this deep desire and drive for a sense of importance, significance and relevance is the cause and the motivator of all human behavior and conflict. This passion for significance knows no boundaries. Rich and poor are victims of its power. King and peasant suffer under its rule. Is this passion for a meaningful life a negative craving? Absolutely not!

This yearning for relevance and significance is evidence of an internal vacuum in the nature of mankind that needs to be filled. This age-old passion is the pursuit of purpose, a relentless reaching for a reason for the gift of life.

In Pursuit of Purpose was written as a result of my long pursuit and ultimate discovery of my purpose in life. I have come to realize the fundamental nature of this search for every man, woman, youth and child, and have, therefore, set forth some of the essential principles, precepts and concepts that you must understand as you embark or continue on your journey of discovering your purpose. *Remember, purpose is the only source of individual and corporate fulfillment.* Join me on a journey that I know you will enjoy. It will make you ask yourself some deep, searching questions, it will challenge your resolve, and it will encourage you to check your definitions of life, success and effectiveness. Come, let us begin our *pursuit of purpose.*

Introduction

"Let me go. Please let me die," sobbed the frail, old gentleman as the strong young swimmer struggled against the boisterous waves of the open ocean.

"Just a few more minutes, sir, and I will have you safely to shore," replied the young man, gasping for every breath.

Finally they made it to the beach and both fell, desperately exhausted, onto the sand. "Why did you save me?" cried the angry seventy-six-year-old man. "Why didn't you let me die? Your good deed is the curse of my existence."

Startled by these words, the young man looked down at the older man who had nearly drowned. As he panted from the heroic effort of rescuing the victim from the violent waves, he shook his head, revealing the shock and the mystification that filled his mind.

Winston had known Mr. Cambridge for twenty years. He had always admired the hard-working businessman for his success. To him, Mr. Cambridge was a role model that embodied all he hoped to be some day. Having worked all his life to achieve the status of being the wealthiest man in the city, Mr. Cambridge owned millions of dollars worth of investments and an enviable mansion on the beach front. He was the father of three well-educated children who all worked in his companies and the husband of a woman who loved him. Hundreds of friends, relatives and admirers looked to him for inspiration and guidance. Perplexed by the disparity between his observations of Mr. Cambridge's life and the gentleman's desire to die, Winston asked, "But, sir. Why do you want to die?" Little did Winston know that the answer to this question would change his life forever. (It may change yours as well.)

As tears flooded his aged eyes, the old man buried his face in his hands and lamented, "What was it all for? Is this all there is? What did I gain? I have everything and yet nothing. Everyone thinks I am a success, but I am a failure. I have given everything and received nothing. I made my parents happy and proud of me, and my wife has everything she could desire. My children want for nothing, and my reputation among my friends, associates and enemies is impressive. Still I am empty, depressed, frustrated and sad. My life has no meaning. Unlike my bank accounts, which are well filled, I am unfulfilled.

"Everyone knows *what* I am, but I still don't know *why* I am. For years I have been so driven by the expectations of others that I have not discovered my personal reason for being. I do not wish to live with such emptiness. Today I decided it was better to be dead than to be alive and not know *why*."

These words pierced the younger man's soul. As he attempted to regain his composure, the old man took his hand, looked into his eyes with a soul-searching gaze and said, "Son, do not strive to be like me. Find out who you are and *be yourself*."

As the medics carried the old man away and the sound of the ambulance faded in the distance, young Winston stood staring out to sea. He was not really aware of his surroundings, for the old man's words had stirred him deeply. "Who am I? What does it mean to be myself?" echoed in his brain.

These questions—Who am I? Why am I here? Where did I come from? What was I born to do? What can I do? Where do I fit? Why am I different? What is my potential? Where am I going? Why did I come to this planet?—are universal questions that haunt every human being. Each of us must find the answers to these questions of purpose if we are going to enjoy a meaningful, effective, fulfilling life.

Purpose is the key to life. Without purpose, life has no meaning. There are millions today just like Mr. Cambridge. They are busy making a living, but they experience very little of life. If your goal in life is to be wealthy so you can retire, you have embarked on a depressing journey to nowhere. *If your vision for life is measured by status, your upkeep will be your downfall.* Vision is buried in purpose. Without knowledge of purpose, life becomes an endless string of activities with little or no significance. Like a rider on a rocking horse, life without purpose makes much motion but no progress.

A World Without Purpose

A lack of purpose and the impending tragedy that results from its absence is found not only in people but in all things. When elements of nature lose their purpose, chaos and destruction are the results. When nations, societies, communities, organizations, friendships, marriages, clubs, churches, countries or tribes lose their sense of purpose and significance, then confusion, frustration, discouragement, disillusionment and corporate suicide—whether gradual or instant—reign. *Purpose is the master of motivation and the mother of commitment.* It is the source of enthusiasm and the womb of perseverance. *Purpose gives birth to hope and instills the passion to act.* It is the common denominator that gives every creature an element of distinction. This guiding sense of purpose is more than an orientation toward a goal. Rather, it is a deep awareness that a common vision encompasses all life and existence. Without this vision, we can only exist. We feel no passion for living, neither do we have a reason to wake up in the morning.

Thousands of years ago, a king known as the wisest man who ever lived stated, "Meaningless! Meaningless! ... Utterly meaningless! Everything is meaningless" (Ecclesiastes 1:2). This was his conclusion after years of observing man's life, activities, plans and achievements apart from a sense of personal and corporate purpose. These words and their sad echo have returned to haunt us nearly six thousand years later. We face a world that acts like a spaceship that has lost its flight plan.

Planet earth is like a mother whose children have lost all sense of direction and all value in life. Globally speaking, everything is in motion. Mergers and acquisitions, deregulations and changing agencies of control, information technologies and international competition all alter the shape and thrust of our economies and the way we do business. Changing demographics, realigned industry structures, new strategic alliances, innovative technologies, unaccustomed modes of working and the volatility of stock markets demand a fresh approach to commerce. Increasing competition, the shrinking of the world into one large global village, the move toward freer markets in former communist countries, and the proposed reality of the European

Common Market alter the way we deal with the world and it deals with us. Many industrialized nations are being transformed into Third World states as numerous people migrate from undeveloped nations.

Long-established ideologies are evaporating in the fires of revolutionary changes. Institutions long held sacred are crumbling under the weight of social pressure. In almost every nation, the situation is the same. There is political confusion, ideological frustration, social unrest, economic uncertainty, moral bankruptcy, institutionalized corruption and disillusionment with religion. All inhabit an environment of fragile diplomacy.

The world has become an incubator of stress, depression, hopelessness and fear. It seems that the kingdoms and the governments of this world are bankrupt. They no longer offer innovative solutions for these ever-increasing problems. Industrialized nations are as fragile as Third World nations. The tremendous changes in national and international situations, and the economic, political, social and cultural transitions that have accompanied these changes, now present a totally different global equation.

There is also a generation in every nation that seems to have lost its sense of purpose. They are out of touch with the values, morals and convictions that build strong families, secure communities, healthy societies and prosperous nations. Thus, the moral fabric of most societies is being stretched and tested to its outer limits. In every nation, the concern is the same. Many of the time-weathered institutions of the industrial states are being tried by challenges that threaten to transform tradition and demand creative and innovative responses.

The dynamic nature of the Third World and the developing countries, because of the infancy of their institutions and their industrial base, are even more hard-pressed to respond effectively to this changing global environment. Political, civic, economic and religious world leaders are perplexed as they see their social infrastructure cracking under the weight of these demands of the new, complex society. A strange sense of insecurity, confusion and aimlessness accompanies these modifications.

History shows that the value of life decreases and the quality of existence diminishes when a generation loses its sense of destiny and purpose. A quick glance at our current world exposes a sad picture that demands our attention. We preserve nature, for example, but kill babies. We build solid houses but cannot construct lasting homes. We are smarter but not wiser, bigger but not stronger. We know more but understand less, and we live longer but enjoy life less fully. We write more books but fail to take the time to read them. We go faster but get nowhere, conquer space but cannot conquer our habits, protect whales but abuse our children, go to the moon but wander far from home, and flirt with fantasy to avoid reality.

The United States of America, the greatest nation in recent history, has come to a crossroads because of a lack of national purpose. Warren Bonnie, distinguished professor of business administration at the University of Southern California, stated in his book *On Becoming a Leader*,

> **"America lost its edge because it lost its way. We forgot what we were here for. We talked about freedom and democracy, but we practiced license and anarchy... As a nation cannot survive without public virtue, it can't progress without a common vision. America hasn't had a national sense of purpose since the 1960s, when, in an unprecedented show of common cause, millions of Americans vehemently opposed government policies."**

Professor Bonnie's words echo an ancient saying written by King Solomon: "Where there is no revelation [vision], the people cast off restraint..." (Proverbs 29:18) With the demise of communism in eastern Europe, the last source of national purpose for America has evaporated. The "red" threat of the bear and the cold war no longer provide the common cause for national commitment that every nation needs.

King Solomon's words contain principles that every living thing should heed. *Where there is no purpose, there is no self-control, no moral conviction and no ethical boundaries.* This principle is increasingly evident in both our personal and corporate lives. America spends more money annually on drugs than on oil. The "Land of the Free and the Home of the Brave" has become the world's number one addict.

Professor Bonnie further contends that "the moment we decided we could create our own reality, we had no use for dreams, forgetting that a dreamless sleep is death." The famous television producer/writer Norman Lear, when commenting on the disillusionment in America said, "The societal disease of our time is short-term thinking." In essence, we have lost our long-term vision and our sense of destiny. Where there is no purpose, no internal reason for living, no significance in life, the demand for discipline, commitment, self-control and respect for authority will gradually diminish until we, like Mr. Cambridge, will sit among our life-long accomplishments and cry with regret, "Is this all there is?"

In more than twenty-five years of working with people in businesses, universities, governments, churches, schools, marriages and families, I have met countless individuals who have achieved an incredible degree of success but have found themselves struggling with an inner hunger that revealed a deep need for personal fulfillment and a yearning for individual significance. This feeling of emptiness and internal failure even after a significant measure of material and social success is a direct result of the failure to discover purpose in life and a reason for being born. Until this direction is discovered, life remains an experiment that is based on assumptions and hypotheses.

You must realize that *your fulfillment in life is dependent on your becoming and doing what you were born to be and do.* Anything less makes life your enemy and death your friend. It is essential, vital, crucial and necessary that you understand this fundamental principle of purpose and pursue it with all your heart. *For without purpose, life has no heart.* Remember, those who don't know where they are going will probably end up someplace else.

Therefore I do not run like a man running aimlessly;
I do not fight like a man beating the air.
1 Corinthians 9:26

CHAPTER ONE

Understanding Purpose

Until purpose is discovered, existence has no meaning, for purpose is the source of fulfillment.

It was the moment for which everyone had been waiting all evening. The thunderous applause of the excited crowd filled the air after the mayor made the announcement, "Ladies and gentlemen, it gives me great pleasure to present the annual Outstanding Citizen of the Year award to Dr. Clyde Wilson, Jr., for his distinguished service to this community."

A well-built, clean-cut young man rose to his feet and walked confidently toward the stage. Sitting at the table he had left were his father, Mr. Clyde Wilson, Sr., and his mother, Emily. This was the moment for which they had waited all their lives—to see their son become all *they* had ever envisioned for him. As pride filled their hearts, they knew that no one in the room could understand their sense of accomplishment, satisfaction and fulfillment.

Mr. Wilson had always dreamed of being a medical doctor. While his son was still quite young, the father had told him that he would do whatever it took to see that the son could become the doctor the father had never been. Young Clyde's parents had labored at many jobs over the years and had lived without the conveniences of life just to make it possible for their son to attend medical school and to complete his internship. This evening made those sacrifices worthwhile, as Clyde junior now brought honor and respect to the family.

As Dr. Wilson stood on stage, holding the plaque, the crowd rose to their feet. Cameras flashed and shouts of adulation filled the room. Then, as the applause subsided, silence filled the room. Everyone waited for the response of the good doctor. For a moment he stood erect, poised to speak. Then his composure broke and, with tears flooding his eyes, the young doctor pleaded with his parents in a loud voice that mirrored the despair in his eyes, "Please, Mom and Dad, forgive me. I am sorry, but I can't go on."

Bewildered and embarrassed by the moment, the chairman helped the doctor off the stage. The crowd stood in questioning shock. What could possibly be stealing this great moment from this successful individual?

As Clyde and his parents drove home that evening, Clyde attempted to explain to his perplexed parents the cause of his uncontrollable behavior. As his words spilled over one another, he tried to describe the frustration that had built within him over the past ten years. "Everything I have accomplished and achieved during these years has been done to please you, Dad, and to fulfill your life-long dreams. I have become what you wanted me to be, but I have never become who I am," he said. "In spite of all the cars, homes and other material things I now have, my life is empty. I never wanted to be a doctor like you did, Dad. In truth, I hate being a doctor. I always wanted to be a musician, but you and Mom would not allow me to follow that dream.

"Please understand. I love and respect you deeply. I know all you have sacrificed to provide me with my education, and I thank you for it. But tonight I realized that I cannot continue living to fulfill your dreams and expectations. I must start fulfilling my own. When I accepted that award tonight, I felt like a hypocrite. Someone I don't even know earned that award because I don't know myself. *I want to live. I want to come alive. I want to be what I was born to be. Please set me free and let me live.*"

There are millions of Clyde Wilson juniors in our world. Perhaps you are one of them. They are busy, active, dedicated, faithful, famous people who are accepted, respected, revered and admired. But deep inside, they are tired, frustrated, bored, disillusioned, confused, empty and depressed. Their lives are aimless. Day after day they go on smiling, pretending and living up to an identity and a reputation that is different from their true selves. The lie they live and the inner yearning to be freed from the tyranny that binds them are a constant source of internal conflict. Whether black, brown, yellow, red or white, you and I are pulled by destiny toward a meaningful, fulfilling life. This human need for personal meaning and satisfaction is universal. Each of us must discover this personal purpose and pursue it relentlessly, or we will fail to live a rich, whole, meaningful life.

Success Without Fulfillment

Human beings, no matter who they are or where they live, all want to be "successful." This success is usually defined by the superficial rewards that are so glorified by the media: wealth, power, fame, luxury and prestige. The goal of material achievement is drilled into us from an early age. Parents urge their children to work hard so they can be "somebody."

Schools add to the pressure by using competitive grading and by offering rewards for outstanding performances. Bookstores are loaded with manuals that instruct readers how to get to the top of their fields so they can accumulate power, wealth and influence, and magazines, complete with cover photos that glamorize the rich and the famous, boldly promise shortcuts to success.

This relentless pursuit of "success" has produced some unglamorous results. Divorce and suicide rates continually climb. Violence, environmental destruction and white collar crime plague every community. Emotional depression, particularly in men and women between the ages of twenty-five and forty-four, has multiplied tenfold over the last two generations. *The internal benchmarks that denote personal and corporate fulfillment are noticeably missing from our world, and a positive sense of direction that encompasses the totality of life is obviously lacking for the majority of people.*

This poverty of satisfaction and meaningful existence is no small matter. A professional career and a large bank account cannot provide these absent ingredients. No amount of accomplishments can replace the power and the motivation of finding your own special niche and working toward your dreams. Inner emptiness is the lot of those who lack a clarity of purpose or those who struggle to live up to someone else's definition of success, be it that of a parent, a spouse, a boss or society in general. Reaching the top of the professional or social ladder is meaningless if it sacrifices personal gratification and well-being.

> **No amount of accomplishments can replace the power and the motivation of finding your own special niche and working toward your dreams.**

As children, we learned to see academic, professional and financial achievements as good, and failures of any kind as bad. Thus, the measures of achievement we received from the previous generations have always been outwardly directed. Success in the eyes of others has been assumed to be personal success, for acclaim from others is the accepted requirement for receiving the "successful" label.

In many cases, the acclaim of others and our personal assessment do not match. Too often, personal satisfaction has been sacrificed to the societal norm of making coincidence, imitation and economic urgency, rather than aptitude, passion and a sense of individual purpose, the basis for critical career decisions. In this, our world has missed the item of true value. *Career success does not automatically yield the desired end of personal fulfillment, which is the only true measure of success.* Private disillusionment and despair characterize many who have allowed the prescriptions of society to dictate their lives. Fulfilling purpose must be the primary goal of every person. Without a commitment to that purpose, there can be no lasting success.

> **Fulfilling purpose must be the primary goal of every person.**

What Is Purpose?

Everything in life has a purpose. Everyone on this planet was born with and for a purpose. It is this *purpose* that is the only source of meaning. *Without purpose, life is an experiment or a haphazard journey that results in frustration, disappointment and failure. Without purpose, life is subjective, or it is a trial and error game that is ruled by environmental influences and the circumstances of the moment. Likewise, in the absence of purpose, time has no meaning, energy has no reason and life has no precision.* Therefore, it is essential that we understand and discover our purpose in life so that we can experience an effective, full and rewarding life.

Purpose is...
...the original intent for the creation of a thing,
...the original reason for the existence of a thing,
...the end for which the means exist,
...the cause for the creation of a thing,
...the desired result that initiates production,
...the need that makes a manufacturer produce a specific product,
...the destination that prompts the journey,
...the expectation of the source,
...the objective for the subject,
...the aspiration for the inspiration, and
...the object one wills or resolves to have.

Purpose, therefore, is the original intent in the mind of the creator that motivated him to create a particular item. It is the *why* that explains the *reason* for existence. Every product is a child of purpose. In other words, before any product is made, there is a purpose established in the mind of the manufacturer that gives conception to the *idea* that becomes the substance for the design and production of the product. Thus, *purpose precedes production.*

Every product is produced by *purpose* for *a purpose.* It exists for its original purpose and thus can find its true fulfillment only in performing the purpose for which it was created. *Until purpose is discovered, existence has no meaning.*

Let us consider, for example, an electric fan. If it were possible for us to enter the mind of the person who invented this product, we might see a desire or an intent to circulate or move air, thus producing a cooling effect. This intent would be established both as the desired end or result and the predetermined purpose for the product, which is the first stage of production.

After the purpose of the product has been determined, the second stage of production follows, which is the development of a design to produce the function that will fulfill the purpose. The design dictates the necessary components and materials for production, which is then incorporated into the product's specifications. When all the drawings, specifications and designs are completed and the materials have been procured, production can begin.

It is essential to note that the production of the product does not begin until the purpose for the product has been established, and the success of the project is not determined until the product does exactly what its purpose requires. Thus, all things begin and end with purpose.

All things begin and end with purpose.

This principle pervades all creation. Nature abounds with evidence of this eternal law. The Master Manufacturer of all created things has made all His creations for a definite purpose and has established that purpose as the ultimate definition of success. You and I are products of His purposeful creating.

Your Purpose Is an Integral Part of You

Like the manufacturer who created the electric fan for a specific purpose, so God created you with a definite purpose in mind. Your existence is evidence that this generation needs something that your life contains. You are the creation that can meet God's desired result.

> **Your existence is evidence that this generation needs something that your life contains.**

Consummating that purpose does not just happen as a by-product of life. You are responsible for the intentional fulfillment of your purpose so the world may benefit from your contribution, just like millions of people are benefiting from the purpose of the electric fan. In essence, you were born *for* a purpose and *with* a purpose. *Your personal fulfillment is possible only in so far as you complete your destiny.* The discovery of your personal purpose and its relationship to God's universal purpose must be the basis from which you live. *You must strive to be who you were born to be.*

As you discover who you are, you will learn that your purpose, your identity, your uniqueness and your potential are interdependent. You cannot truly "know thyself," as the great Greek philosophers admonished, until you discover your purpose. This is true because known purpose reveals the particular components God built into you to enable you to achieve all that He prepared for you.

Nothing is truly yours until you understand it—not even yourself. Some people are born knowing what they want to do and even how to do it. The rest of us must spend hours figuring out what to do with our lives. Vague goals such as "I want to be happy," "I want to make the world a better place to live," or even "I want to be rich" are nearly useless. We must ask the primary question—*"Why am I here?"*—and reply with an unqualified answer—*"To be myself and to express myself fully."*

Concern for doing the right thing rather than a desire to do things right must always guide you. That right thing is the purpose for which God created you and gave you breath. You are special and unique. God made you from an original mold, then threw it away when you were completed.

Check out your uniqueness and find out what differentiates you from the billions of people who inhabit this planet. Then pursue your aspiration deliberately and consistently. Be what you are. Capitalize on the natural skills and talents with which you were born, and don't lose them. When others belittle your special gifts and try to remake you according to their plans and purposes, refuse to yield to their domination. Don't let anyone prevent you from becoming and doing all that you were born to be and do. Remember, if you don't deploy yourself, others will soon employ you. Above all else, pursue purpose with a passion and experience the reason for your life.

The purposes of a man's heart are deep waters, but a man of understanding draws them out.
Proverbs 20:5

❖ **PRINCIPLES** ❖

1. The human need for personal meaning and satisfaction is universal.

2. Personal fulfillment is the only true measure of success.

3. Fulfilling purpose must be the primary goal of every person.

4. Everything in life has a purpose.

5. Purpose is the original intent in the mind of the creator that motivated him to create a particular item.

6. Purpose always precedes production.

7. All things begin and end with purpose.

8. God created you with a definite purpose in mind.

CHAPTER TWO

The Nature
of
Purpose

Plans may change, but purpose is constant.

When a child opens a package and finds a new toy that is not familiar to her, she will either sit and look at it for a while, trying to figure it out, or she will take it to her mommy or daddy and ask, "What it this? How does it work?" In both cases she is trying to determine the nature of the toy—what makes it fun to play with. This desire to understand the nature of something is an important part of learning.

The nature of a thing, by definition, is the "particular combination of qualities belonging to a person, animal, thing or class by birth, origin or constitution" or "the instincts or inherent tendencies that direct its conduct." Thus, a study of the nature of purpose will reveal both the qualities that belong to purpose and the inherent tendencies that affect its behavior. Understanding the nature of purpose is an important prelude to discovering God's purpose for our lives.

Purpose Is Inherent

When a manufacturer creates a new product, he lets the product's intended use govern the design, function and nature of the product so that the fulfillment of its purpose is inseparably built into it. Purpose predicts the nature of something, and nature is that which a product inherently is. Nature is always given for the express purpose of executing the manufacturer's reason for creating the product.

Say, for example, that a manufacturer wants to make something that will move products from one place to another. Before the machine can fulfill its purpose, the manufacturer must decide how it will move things. Then he must design that ability into the machine. The purpose of the machine thus becomes an inseparable part of its existence, because its ability to move things is built into the belts and the rollers of the design, which permits it to fulfill its intended use.

When God creates men and women, He designs them to fulfill their function and gives them certain qualities and characteristics that enable them to perform His intended purpose. These abilities are yours before birth. They do not come to you when you receive Jesus and are reborn.

Thus, your natural inclinations to socialize with people or to seek solitude, to think with your mind or to do things with your hands, to communicate with words or to express yourself through the various art forms, to come up with the ideas or to put them into action, to lead or to follow, to inspire or to manage, to calculate or to demonstrate are part of your makeup and your personality from the time God chose to make you and designed you in a particular way. They relate to your purpose, which is a natural, innate, intimate part of who you are. You are designed for your purpose. You are perfect for your purpose.

> **You are designed for your purpose.**
> **You are perfect for your purpose.**

Your purpose, your abilities and your outlook on life cannot be separated, because your purpose determines how you will function, which establishes how you are designed, which is related to your potential, which is connected to your natural abilities. *To remove your purpose would be to significantly change who you are, because your purpose both informs and reveals your nature and your responsibilities. Everything you naturally have and inherently are is necessary for you to fulfill your purpose. Your height, race, skin color, language, physical features and intellectual capacity are all designed for your purpose.*

If, for example, I decided that my hair dryer didn't need any air vents on the side, I would destroy its ability to dry my hair. Because the hair dryer's purpose of drying hair requires that it function by blowing out warm or hot air, which dictates its design, my closing the vents would prevent the dryer from doing its thing. With no way to draw in air to be heated and blown back out, the dryer's existence would be meaningless. The hair dryer's purpose would be the same, but its ability to fulfill that purpose would have changed.

This is why it is very important and essential that you never try to become like someone else. You can and should learn from others, but you must never become them. You can never fulfill your purpose without being yourself. Who and what you are is important and essential to why you are. *Purpose is why.*

Never try to become like someone else.

In new birth, God reclaims what is rightfully His. He redirects the natural skills and abilities that satan perverted and employs them for the completion of His plans and purposes. Taking away what is destroying you, He encourages you to rediscover all those things that you like to do. As He restores His anointing on your life, the power to perform with excellence reinstates the beauty and the perfection of your innate abilities. Then He says, "Go ahead. Do all you like to do for My glory and the advancement of My Kingdom."

The biblical character of Moses is a good example of the inherent nature of purpose. Moses was a man with a deliverance instinct. He was born to be a deliverer. Even before he met God, he wanted to set people free. One day he saw an Egyptian beating a Hebrew. When no one was looking, he killed the Egyptian and hid him in the sand. The next day he saw two Hebrews fighting. When he asked one of them, "Why are you hitting your fellow Hebrew?" the man replied, "Who made you ruler and judge over us? Are you thinking of killing me as you killed the Egyptian?" (Exodus 2:13-14)

When Moses heard this, he became afraid and fled to a nearby country where he shepherded his father-in-law's sheep (Exodus 2:1-3:1). Years later, God reclaimed for His own purposes the deliverance and leadership skills that He had given to Moses. He sent Moses to the Pharoah of Egypt to free the Israelites from slavery (Exodus 3:10).

God didn't throw away the skills and the talents that had been with Moses from birth, He simply renewed them and redirected them to their intended use. The purpose of

Moses' life didn't change; the use of the gifts that fulfilled his purpose were simply redirected toward the purpose for which they had been given. Those same gifts God had given Moses at birth—basic components of his makeup—brought freedom to the Israelites and glory to God. In essence, Moses was equipped for his purpose, and so are you.

Purpose Is Individual

The individual nature of purpose is best seen in the various parts of a product. Each has a unique function and design that enables it to meet the manufacturer's reason for including it in the product. This uniqueness doesn't make the various parts unequal, just different. In other words, you are the *way* you are because of *why* you are.

> **You are the *way* you are because of *why* you are.**

When an electronics manufacturer, for example, creates a stereo system, he may include a turntable, a cassette player and a CD player to fulfill different purposes that are not interchangeable. The turntable cannot play a cassette tape, neither can the CD player produce music from a record. Their purposes are individual and separate, though they are similar and related.

This same principle applies to men and women. God needs you because your purpose is unique. He's designed you specifically to meet His requirements. No one has your fingerprint, your personality or your particular combination of natural skills and talents. Oh, they may look like you, but they aren't you, because there's a part of God only you can express. *In essence, there is something you came to this planet to do that the world needs in this generation. Your birth is evidence that your purpose is necessary.*

> **Your birth is evidence that your purpose is necessary.**

This uniqueness of purpose is evident in the lives of two great leaders in history, the apostles Peter and Paul. Their corporate purposes were the same. Both were given the task of reconciling mankind to their Creator and spreading the Good News of the Kingdom of God. Beyond that, their purposes were different.

Peter, after the vision that led him to the house of Cornelius (Acts 10), related primarily to the church in Jerusalem. His purpose was to be a leader among the Jewish believers, convincing them that God was also incorporating Gentiles into the Church by the gift of His Spirit (Acts 2, 11). Paul, on the other hand, was rarely in Jerusalem. His visits there were for the primary purpose of defending His ministry among the Gentiles to those same leaders that Peter influenced.

> ...they saw that I had been entrusted with the task of preaching the gospel to the Gentiles, just as Peter had been to the Jews. For God, who was at work in the ministry of Peter as an apostle to the Jews, was also at work in my ministry as an apostle to the Gentiles (Galatians 2:7-8).

Paul's purpose or reason for being born was to specifically go to the non-Jewish world and share the good news of reconciliation to God. The apostle Peter was called to oversee the church in the Jerusalem. Both shared in the spread of the gospel, but their purposes were separate and specific. They could not have changed places and remained true to God's purposes for their lives. The same is true for you. *No one can take your place or purpose, and for you there is no substitute.*

Purpose Is Often Multiple

Just as purpose is specific to a particular individual or product, even so that purpose may be varied and numerous. As we have seen, God gave the lights He placed in the sky a variety of purposes. The sun, for example, was created to 1) separate the day from the night, 2) mark the seasons, days and years, 3) govern the day, 4) separate light from darkness, and 5) give light to the earth (Genesis 1:14-18).

This multiple purpose is visible throughout creation. Trees give us oxygen, shade and fruit; animals provide food and clothing; flowers beautify the earth, satisfy the bees' need for nectar and supply pollen for the production of fruit; and men and women assume the varied roles of spouse, parent, worker, church member and friend.

This variety of purpose is again evident in the life of Moses. Moses was a spokesman for God to the Pharoah of Egypt (Exodus 3-13), the warrior of God, who by his uplifted hands brought victory over the Amalekites (Exodus 17:8-13), the priest of God, who mediated between God and His people (Exodus 19-31), the servant of God, who interceded for an idolatrous people (Exodus 32:1-14), and the lawgiver of God, who authored the first five books of the Bible.

With the multiplication of purpose always comes different scopes of vision, which require varied actions and responses. Moses was both confidant and judge, suiting his actions and responses to meet the purpose he was fulfilling. Knowing and understanding the variety of purposes that had claims on his life influenced how well he fulfilled his overall purpose as the leader of God's people. In some respects, his ability to meet the demands of this multiplicity of purpose was made possible by the interdependent nature of purpose. He needed Joshua, Jethro and others to help him carry out his God-given purpose.

You were born *with* and *for* a purpose. However, that purpose may incorporate many minor facets whose purposes or intents are to fulfill the greater, overall purpose for your life.

> **You were born *with* and *for* a purpose.**

Purpose Is Interdependent

Everything has a particular purpose that is linked to a greater purpose. Or to say it another way, everything has a purpose larger than its specific end so that every individual purpose is fulfilled only when the personal task is pursued within the scope of the greater purpose and for its fulfillment. *Nothing exists for itself; everything is related to something else.*

The moon provides a good example of the interdependent nature of purpose. When God created lights and placed them in the sky, He made a greater light, the sun, and a lesser light, the moon. The sun was given the task of ruling the day and the moon was designed to govern the night.

The moon is not created to shine—it has no light of its own—but to reflect light like a large mirror. Thus, the moon catches the light of the sun and sends it back to the side of the earth that is away from the sun, providing light in the night. That's why the moon rotates in a certain position all year. Although it appears differently to us on any given night of the month, the moon's position does not change. To fulfill its purpose, the moon must always remain in a position to catch the sun's light and reflect it to the earth.

It also follows that the sun and the earth must remain in position for the moon to fulfill its purpose. If the earth leaves its designated rotation around the sun or tilts on its axis farther than God's design intended, the moon cannot do what it was created to do.

Or take a battery. The purpose of a battery is to store energy until it is needed. If the battery is never placed into a position that requires its stored energy, it cannot fulfill its purpose. The satisfaction of its purpose is related to its position in a product that has a larger purpose.

So a car battery cannot fulfill its purpose unless you turn the key in the ignition and allow the battery to send power to the engine, which starts the engine that powers the wheels that move the car. Without all the other parts, neither the battery, the engine, the wheels nor the car can fulfill their purposes. Everything needs something.

The world needs you and the purpose for which you were born. You also need the purposes of others in order to fulfill your purpose. Purpose cannot be fulfilled in isolation.

Purpose cannot be fulfilled in isolation.

This same phenomenon of interdependent purpose is evident in the Church. The apostle Paul uses the image of the body to describe this interrelatedness.

> Just as each of us has one body with many members, and these members do not all have the same function, so in Christ we who are many form one body, and each member belongs to all the others (Romans 12:4-5).

...God has combined the members of the body and has given greater honor to the parts that lacked it, so that there should be no division in the body, but that its parts should have equal concern for each other. If one part suffers, every part suffers with it; if one part is honored, every part rejoices with it. Now you are the body of Christ, and each one of you is a part of it (1 Corinthians 12:24-27).

Thus, we see that the interrelatedness of the Church is part of God's purpose. He gives to each member a task that contributes to the Church's overall purpose, thereby allowing the Church to grow and build "itself up in love, as each part does its work" (Ephesians 4:16). Nothing exists for itself. Everything is part of a larger purpose.

Can you imagine? Not even God could fulfill His purpose without the cooperation of His creation. Just suppose the tree on which Jesus died had refused to become a tree or if Joseph of Arimathea had not purchased the tomb in which Jesus was destined to lay. Your purpose is designed to affect history within and beyond your generation. *You are a necessary part of the world's population and a vital link in this generation. We need your purpose.*

Purpose Is Permanent

Many are the plans in a man's heart, but it is the Lord's purpose that prevails (Proverbs 19:21).

God has also given purpose the quality of permanence. Once a manufacturer designs, produces and markets a product that fulfills a certain purpose, he doesn't change that purpose because a consumer doesn't like the way it works. He may change the design or the components or the materials used in the components, but he will not change the purpose, because the purpose behind the product is what gives it meaning. In other words, plans might change, but purpose is constant. *What* God wants is established, but *how* He gets it may vary.

> ***What* God wants is established, but *how* He gets it may vary.**

This quality of purpose combats the many plans and schemes that we come up with to meet our God-intended reason for life. The Book of Genesis describes both God's promise to Abraham and Sarah that they would have a son, and Sarah's frantic efforts to help God achieve that purpose when the years rolled by and she had not yet given birth to a son. Giving her maid Hagar to Abraham, she hoped to have a son through her.

When Hagar conceived and bore a son, whom Abraham named Ishmael, Abraham tried to make him the promised son. But God did not accede to his wishes. God had promised Abraham a son through his wife Sarah, and that remained God's promise, because His purpose as revealed in His covenant with Abraham was that Sarah would be the mother of the promised son (Genesis 17:17-22).

Purpose Is Resilient

Related to the quality of permanence is the characteristic of resiliency in purpose. When a manufacturer sets a purpose for a product and develops a plan to achieve that purpose, no amount of problems with the manufacturing process will change the product's purpose. No matter how bad things become, the manufacturer will not say, "We're having trouble getting this product to do what we want it to do, so let's have it do this instead."

Each difficulty that seeks to hinder progress toward the completion of a product that fulfills the manufacturer's original intent is used to learn more about the product and the way it must naturally function to carry out its purpose. The journey may include bumps and detours, but eventually it will come to the desired end. In other words, no matter how bad the process becomes, the manufacturer uses the problems for good as he incorporates the insight gained from the challenges to build a superior product that does all it's supposed to do.

If you have made decisions that have interfered with God's plan and purpose for your life, He has arranged a reformation program to redeem the detours. He uses the experiences to refine you as a purposeful part of the whole. Purpose transforms mistakes into miracles and disappointments into testimonies.

> **Purpose transforms mistakes into miracles and disappointments into testimonies.**

This resiliency of purpose is evident in the lives of many people who have missed their purpose. They had great talent, but they didn't know what they were supposed to do with it. I think of the apostle Paul. He intrigues me. Paul, or Saul as he was known before he met Christ on the road to Damascus, was a very talented person.

First, Paul was a great organizer. He both organized the systematic persecution of the church in Jerusalem and received letters of introduction from the Jewish high priest that permitted him to persecute the followers of Jesus in Damascus (Acts 8:3; 9:1). Secondly, he was a leader, as was evident in his role in the stoning of Stephen:

> **When the blood of your martyr Stephen was shed, I stood there giving my approval and guarding the clothes of those who were killing him** (Acts 22:20; see also Acts 7:58; 8:1).

Third, Paul was a skilled tentmaker who liked to work with his hands (Acts 18:3). Fourth, Paul was a communicator. By speaking and by writing, Paul declared what he believed. (Much of the New Testament is the result of his communication skills.)

Although Paul's natural talents and skills were initially used in opposition to his God-given task of carrying the Good News of Jesus to the Gentiles, his purpose did not change. *God changed his name but not his purpose.* Purpose remains true no matter what path a person or a thing takes to achieve its intended goal.

God's purpose is not hindered by your past. He turned a coward (Gideon) into a mighty leader (Judges 6-8), and a murderer (Moses) into a deliverer (Exodus 3). He also turned a prostitute (the Samaritan woman Jesus met at the well of Jacob) into a preacher (John 4:1-42). Imagine what He could make of you. You are not too old to resume your purpose. Nothing you have done can cancel your purpose. The world is waiting for you to produce your purpose.

God's purpose is not hindered by your past.

Purpose Is Universal

No manufacturer goes to the trouble to design, produce and market a product for which he has no purpose. Who would want a useless thing? Thus, everything has a purpose. Or, to say it another way, the gift of purpose is universal. Nothing is created without a purpose behind the making. This principle is evident in nature.

Every human being, every living thing, indeed everything that exists, has been chosen by God to fulfill His purposes. We all have part of this universal purpose. When God chose the sun, He chose it for a purpose. Then He created it with the ability to complete its purpose. God also chose the mosquito and designed into it everything it needs to fulfill its reason for being. The oceans, too, were created by God to perform the tasks He dictated for them before they were completed. Nothing is outside God's universal purpose. *Whenever this commonness of purpose is not recognized, death occurs.*

The Dead Sea is a good example of the inevitable death that occurs when purpose is not fulfilled. The Dead Sea lies to the south of the Lake (or Sea) of Galilee, with the Jordan River connecting the two. It catches the water coming south, but it doesn't let it out. Like all bodies of water that cease to have a current running through them—both giving and receiving—the Dead Sea is well described by its name. It is just dead water.

When I visited the Dead Sea, our guides instructed us to be very careful that we did not allow a drop of the water to get into our eyes because the water is so salty, it will literally burn a hole into your cornea and you will become blind. When I went into the water, I found that I could not sit down. It was impossible to sink. The salt content gives the water a buoyancy that is unnatural. Also, unlike other bodies of water, the Dead Sea contains no plant or marine life. There are no fish, neither are there algae or other kinds of sea plants. No great creatures of the sea live in its depths, neither do the many living creatures of the sea teem in its water. The water is just too salty to sustain life. Sharing the universality of purpose but failing to live up to that purpose, the sea has died. The lake's purpose hasn't changed, but its ability to perform what God intended has been replaced by death.

In many ways, the tragedy of the Dead Sea is indicative of our lives. God has a universal purpose for mankind that goes beyond our abilities to perform it. Before creation, He predestined us and chose us to be conformed into the image of His Son. He set Christ as our destination, then backed us up and started us on the journey toward that desired end.

Most of humanity has lost sight of our universal purpose. Like the Dead Sea, we are not fulfilling all that God purposed for our lives. That failure to live out all that God put us here to do has not changed God's purpose. His desire to see all men and women know life as He intended it is so strong that He has tried again and again throughout the history of man to redirect us into His predestined path. The life, death and resurrection of Jesus Christ is His final attempt. Through Him we can move from death to life. Through Him we can rediscover our God-given universal purpose.

Not one person on this planet is outside that will of God, for He has chosen each of us to share in His glory. *Thus, no matter how your life started or how bad it has been, you are not a mistake. God intended for you to live, both physically and spiritually. He would not have allowed you to be born if you were not included in His universal purposes. You are necessary. You are essential.*

The universality of purpose is something we can cling to when life becomes meaningless and without value. Together with the intrinsic, individual, multiple, interdependent, permanent and resilient qualities of purpose, it gives us an assurance that we are not mistakes. God had a purpose for us when He planted us in our mothers' wombs. That purpose has not changed. The challenge that lies before us is to understand the basic principles that underlie purpose so we can recognize purpose at work in our lives and allow it to guide and redirect our paths.

Before I formed you in the womb I knew you, before you were born I set you apart...
Jeremiah 1:5

❖ **PRINCIPLES** ❖

1. God's intentions for your life govern
   your design, function and nature.

2. Everything you naturally have and
   inherently are is necessary for you to
   fulfill your purpose.

3. God designed you to meet the unique
   requirements of your purpose.

4. Your purpose may incorporate many
   smaller facets that contribute to God's
   overall purpose for your life.

5. Your individual purpose is linked to a
   greater purpose.

6. The world needs you and the purpose
   for which you were born.

7. Purpose combats the many plans and
   schemes we come up with to help God
   meet His intended reasons for our lives.

8. Purpose remains true no matter what
   path we take to achieve our intended
   goal.

CHAPTER THREE

The Principles of Purpose

Keep your head and your heart going in the right direction, and you will not have to worry about your feet.

Have you ever watched the ocean? The constant ebb and flow of the waves reveals the order with which God created the world. With care and precision He established basic laws and principles that would fulfill His plans and purposes for all creation.

A principle, by definition, is "an accepted or professed rule of action or conduct," "a fundamental, primary, or general law or truth from which others are derived" or "a fundamental doctrine." Thus, principles are fundamental truth with universal application. They govern and reveal the normal operation or behavior of something.

Principles are like lighthouses. They are laws that cannot be broken. We can only break ourselves against them. Just as the Law or Principle of Universal Gravitation both governs and exhibits the attraction between the earth and the moon, and the Law or Principle of Centrifugal Force controls and reveals the behavior of the earth's revolution around the sun, so the principles of purpose both rule and make known the function of purpose. There are seven basic principles that characterize purpose as God designed it.

Principle #1—God is a God of purpose.

Every creator or manufacturer begins with purpose. He first establishes his intent before beginning the process of production. God is the source of purpose. Nature is filled with evidence that He determines the purpose for a thing before He creates it. In other words, God never made anything for the fun of it. He never created something just to see if He could make it. Before the creative act ever takes place, God has in His mind the why and the how of what He decides to make. He does everything *with* and *for* a purpose. Long before God became the Creator, He was planning and designing the many things He would speak into existence.

God never made anything for the fun of it.

The intentional nature of God is also seen throughout His interaction with mankind. He purposed to save Noah from the flood that would destroy the earth before He told Noah to build a boat (Genesis 6:9-22). He established that Esau, the elder son of Isaac, would serve Jacob, the younger son, before Rebekah had given birth to them (Genesis 25:19-26). He ordained that King David's son Solomon would build the Lord a temple long before Solomon was born (2 Samuel 7:1-16; 1 Chronicles 22:6-10). He determined that a virgin would have a child before the Holy Spirit came over Mary (Isaiah 7:14; Matthew 1:18,20-21). And He appointed Paul to be His messenger to the Gentiles before He sent

Ananias to pray for Paul so he could receive his sight again (Acts 9:15).

These and many other examples that have not been cited reveal God's character of acting with purpose. He is a God of purpose. He never acts without first setting the end toward which His actions are directed. God never creates before He purposes. It was His purpose that generated all He created and forever established the intent for everything that exists.

Principle #2—Everything in life has a purpose.

If God is a God of purpose and He created everything, then everything in life has a purpose. This amazes me. When I look at a roach before I kill it or a rat caught in a trap, I wonder that God has a plan and a purpose for each of these creatures. The lice we detest and the snakes we fear were made by God to fulfill a specific purpose, as were mosquitos, birds and trees. God took as much time putting together spiders and ants as He did creating butterflies and flowers. Just because we don't understand a creature's purpose doesn't mean that it is purposeless. Our reactions of fear or disgust do not negate their reasons for existence, because everything serves a purpose. In essence, ignorance of purpose does not cancel purpose.

> **Ignorance of purpose does not cancel purpose.**

Consequently, everything, no matter how insignificant it may seem, exists for a distinct purpose in the mind of God to serve a greater purpose. The hairs in your nostrils were carefully designed by God and intentionally placed there for the purpose of trapping bacteria, germs and dust particles, preventing them from contaminating the lungs during inspiration. The wax in your ears has a purpose.

Your ear glands were created to produce wax to attract and trap dust particles, bacteria and germs before they can enter the delicate inner ear and cause infection. There is nothing in your body that does not serve a vital purpose, even down to the smallest detail.

This is also true of nature. Mankind has recently discovered that every animal and every plant was created to balance the ecosystem. Any disruption in its purpose affects everything else. The ozone layer of the upper atmosphere has recently been discovered to have a critical purpose to perform. It was designed to help preserve life on our planet by regulating the intensity of the ultraviolet rays from the sun. The plants themselves absorb the ultraviolet rays of the sun and produce chlorophyll for their food, while releasing oxygen for us to breathe. Their purpose involves keeping us alive by providing both food and oxygen. We, in turn, inspire oxygen and expire carbon dioxide, which the plant absorbs to make its food. Therefore, we need their purpose and they need ours.

It should also be noted that God created nothing for beauty, even though the things He created are beautiful. Beauty is a by-product of design, not a creature's intended purpose. Thus, if God designed the hairs on a bee's leg to transfer pollen from one flower to another, and placed the hairs in your nostrils and the wax in your ears for a specific purpose, then you must know that He has a purpose for your life.

Principle #3—Not every purpose is known.

Our world is plagued by the desire to have more and more and more. But having something is not really the most important thing. Knowing the reason for what you have is much more important. There are times, however, when the why is not known. This doesn't mean that the thing, event or person doesn't have a purpose; its purpose just isn't known. The story of a man named Jonah shows what can happen when purpose is unknown.

The Book of Jonah describes the adventures of a prophet who didn't want to obey God's command. When God told him to go to the Assyrian capital of Ninevah and preach against their wickedness, Jonah disobeyed. He tried to run away from God by boarding a ship that was sailing in the opposite direction. While they were at sea, a violent storm nearly broke the ship apart. The terrified sailors cried for help and threw the cargo overboard to lessen the danger. Meanwhile, Jonah was sleeping in the hold of the ship.

When the captain found him, he awakened Jonah and told him to pray to his God. The storm continued to rage until the sailors finally decided to draw lots to see who was to blame for the danger. The lot fell on Jonah, who then answered their questions saying, "I am a Hebrew and I worship the Lord, the God of heaven, who made the sea and the land" (Jonah 1:9). Then he described how he was running away from God and told them to throw him into the sea. Because the sailors were reluctant to follow Jonah's suggestion, they tried to row to shore. But the storm became worse. Finally, they threw Jonah overboard and the sea became calm.

The sailors' problem was not the storm, but the unknown purpose of the storm. Had they known earlier that the storm was God's means of talking to Jonah, they wouldn't have wasted so much time trying to save themselves. Their lack of knowledge didn't cancel the storm's purpose. It just meant they didn't have the same information Jonah had. They didn't know the storm's purpose. Unknown purpose always wastes time and gives the possibility of danger.

Principle #4—Wherever purpose is not known, abuse is inevitable.

One day I was washing my car with an old bath towel when my daughter came to me and said, "Dad, what are you doing?" "I'm washing the car," I said, to which she replied, "No, you're using the towel. That's to bathe with." Because she obviously was right, I had to come up with something smart as a response. So I said, "Yes, this towel is designed to bathe with, but we've bathed with it enough. Now it's time for the car to get bathed with it."

Although my daughter accepted my explanation, her concept was good. I was abusing that towel. I wasn't using it for its intended purpose. Abuse occurs whenever we don't use something according to its creator's intentions.

Abuse occurs whenever we don't use something according to its creator's intentions.

In other words, if you don't know the purpose for something (or you choose to ignore that purpose), you can't do anything other than abuse it. No matter how good your intentions may be, they are canceled by your ignorance. You may be sincere and committed toward your husband, your child or your boss, but your sincerity and commitment cannot make up for your lack of knowledge of their purpose. Abuse remains inevitable, and you put them in danger.

Thus, when we run into problems with certain aspects of God's creation, the plant or the animal or the person is not causing the difficulty. It is our use (or abuse) of that plant, animal or person that gets us into a predicament.

The word *abuse* means "abnormal use." Or to say it another way, if you don't know the proper use for something, you will use it in an erratic and disorderly manner. Unknown purpose also leads to *misuse*, which is a stronger form of abuse. To misuse something means that you miss the intended use. Although the product has a purpose, you miss knowing it and thus use it for something other than what the creator had in mind when he designed and made it.

If you don't know the purpose for a baby, you will misuse the child. (We call that child abuse.) If you don't know the purpose for money, you will abuse the money. If you don't know the purpose for a job, you'll misuse the job. If you don't know the purpose for your mate, you'll abuse your spouse. (We call that wife abuse or husband abuse.)

It is therefore very important that you either discover the purpose for everything you encounter in life or refrain from using that person or thing until you gain that knowledge. If, for example, your friend asks you to marry him, but he doesn't know the purpose of marriage, you would be wise to refuse to marry him until he discovers the God-given purpose for marriage. Otherwise, he will abuse both marriage and, as a result, you.

Many of us have been victims because others have abused the very things that God Himself created. That's why it is very important that we not move into marriage, school, a new job, and so forth until we know God's purpose for giving us that relationship or position. It is the violation of this principle that is the cause for all our social problems today. The drug problem is not a substance problem, but a substance abuse problem. We abuse the godly gift of sex and experience the fatal consequences because we don't seek the purpose for these things.

The New Testament tells the story of a man named Simon who lived in Samaria. Simon was a magician who claimed to have great powers. When Peter and John came to Samaria and preached the gospel, he believed their message and was baptized. He remained envious, however, of Peter and John, who were performing many miracles. When he saw them lay hands on believers so they could receive the

Holy Spirit, he offered them money to give him the same powers. Peter rightly rebuked him for trying to buy God's gifts (Acts 8:9-25).

Simon's wrong was not that he wanted to share in the ministry of laying on of hands, but that he wanted the gift for the wrong motive. The Scriptures are clear that God's gifts are given for the good of the whole body (1 Corinthians 10:24; 12:7). Simon sought to abuse God's gifts by using them selfishly. *All abuse is a violation of purpose.*

Principle #5—If you want to know the purpose of a thing, never ask the thing.

Have you ever asked a microphone or a chair or a plant why it exists? Of course not, because they can't possibly tell you what you want to know. The same is true of all things, whether or not they can talk. A created thing can never know what was in the mind of the creator when he planned and built it.

A created thing can never know what was in the mind of the creator when he planned and built it.

As ridiculous as the thought of asking a piano or a stereo why it exists may be, we have been doing that to each other for years. "Hey, what's happening? Why are you here?" Although your friend may respond to your question, it's probably not the right answer because you asked him the wrong question. Asking a friend why you or he exists is like the blind leading the blind. Most men and women don't know why they are here.

You will never find your purpose as long as you ask a creature who you are because a person or thing apart from its creator cannot know its purpose. You may even come up with a purpose that isn't God's purpose and think that you are finally on the right track.

The futility of understanding God's purposes apart from Him is graphically portrayed in the encounter between God and Job in the latter part of the Book of Job. Job was a faithful worshiper of God who lost everything when God agreed that satan could test his faithfulness. Job's friends incessantly speculated, lectured, blamed and argued, trying to decide why Job was experiencing such misfortune. When Job and his friends had ceased talking, God spoke to Job out of a storm. Again and again He questioned Job's understanding of things he could not know because they required knowledge of God's purposes in creation.

> Who are you to question My wisdom with your ignorant, empty words? Stand up now like a man and answer the questions I ask you. Were you there when I made the world? If you know so much, tell Me about it. ... What holds up the pillars that support the earth? ... Have you any idea how big the world is? Answer Me if you know. Do you know where the light comes from or what the source of darkness is? ... Do you know the laws that govern the skies and can you make them apply to the earth? ... Who is wise enough to count the clouds and tilt them over to pour out the rain...? Job, you challenged Almighty God; will you give up now, or will you answer? (Job 38:2-4,6a,18-19,33,37; 40:1-2 GN)

Obviously, Job could not answer because only God could tell him how the world was created to operate and why it was made that way. The rain could not, neither could the light or the darkness. Finally, Job admitted defeat. He would never know the reasons behind his experiences unless God explained them to him, because creatures can never know purpose apart from the creator.

Principle #6—Purpose is only found in the mind of the creator.

I was in an oriental antique store one day that had beautiful furniture and trinkets. As I walked into the store, I picked up four or five bowls of different sizes and shapes. I thought, "These are nice dishes to eat from." So I took them to the attendant and said, "How much are these bowls?"

The attendant, who was Korean, replied adamantly, "These aren't bowls."

"Oh, I'm sorry," I said. "What are they?"

"These are ceremonial dishes for a Korean wedding," he replied.

"Excuse me," I said and replaced the dishes. Then I picked up some sort of thing that flapped and made noise that sounded like music to me and said, "This is a good musical instrument. How much is it?"

Again the attendant replied, "That's not a musical instrument. This is used for incense when you go to the temple."

Again I said, "Excuse me," and continued my search. After I had missed four or five times, I asked him to go with me as I walked through the shop. As we looked at the many interesting items on display, I constantly asked him, "What's this?" "What's that?" "How is this used?" The attendant, who had grown up in Korea, knew the purpose for everything that I asked about. What looked like a stool, for example, was really a chest of drawers. Indeed, it would have broken had I sat on it.

Because he was part of the culture, the clerk knew the purpose for everything in the whole store. He did not need to guess at the purpose of each item like I had done (I was wrong eighty percent of the time), because he knew from experience how each piece was to be used.

Had I simply bought the objects I liked without asking what they were and how they were to be used, I would have ruined some beautiful pieces. Since I didn't know their purpose, abuse was inevitable no matter how sincere I was. My friends and my family would have misused them as well because they wouldn't have been any more knowledgeable concerning the purpose of the item than I was. Just because we all would have used them the same way wouldn't have made our use right. In ignorance, we all would have abused them.

The same principle is true for any product. If you want to know the purpose of a product, you must ask the manufacturer or his authorized representative. The product, itself, cannot tell you. That's why most manufacturers put a label somewhere on their products or they give you similar information in an owner's manual. They want to teach you about the product and give you the opportunity to contact them if you have any questions about its purpose, use, operation or maintenance. They know they must give you this information if the product is going to fulfill the purpose for which they made it.

This principle of asking the creator for the purpose of a thing is also evident in the story of a blind man healed by Jesus. Jesus and His disciples were walking along when they saw a man who had been blind from birth. Jesus' disciples immediately wanted to know why the man had been born blind. Because their tradition said such things were the result of sin, they wanted to know if the man or his parents had sinned. Jesus went straight to the root of the matter. "Neither this man nor his parents sinned...but this happened so that the work of God might be displayed in his life" (John 9:3).

After Jesus had healed him, the blind man was questioned by everyone he met, including the Jewish authorities: "What happened to you?" "Aren't you the blind man who used to beg by the gate?" "Where is this man who healed you?" "Don't you know He's a sinner?" The man didn't attempt to explain why he had been healed, he simply told what he knew. If the Jewish officials and everyone else wanted to know why he had been healed, they would have to ask Jesus like His disciples had, because only the originator of an action knows the purpose behind it. Therefore, if you want to know the purpose of a thing, including yourself, you must discover who created it and submit to his knowledge. Only God knows the purpose for your life.

Only God knows the purpose for your life.

Principle #7—Purpose is the key to fulfillment.

Manufacturers always want the consumer to be satisfied with their product. Labels and instruction books are their way of telling you what they had in mind when they created the product so you can compare that to your expectations when you bought it. If the purpose of the manufacturer and the expectations of the purchaser don't match, the product can't possibly satisfy both the consumer's desires and the manufacturer's objectives. *Purpose dictates performance, which influences satisfaction.* Thus, purpose is the key to fulfillment.

Likewise, your purpose is the key to your life. It tells you what you are supposed to do and why. It reveals the reasons behind life's experiences and demands, and supplies a vision for the future. It also provides a perspective that gives life significance and meaning. Apart from purpose, life seems fatalistic and haphazard, and the events of life become more important than the reasons behind them.

In essence, you will never experience true fulfillment and peace until you are executing the purpose for which you were born. Just like a trumpet's purpose is fulfilled when it is blown, a piano when it is skillfully played, a car when it is safely driven and a seed when it becomes a tree, even so your fulfillment is dependent on your discovering and fulfilling your purpose.

Naaman was a Syrian who had to learn the significance of purpose. One day his wife's servant girl told her mistress that a prophet in Samaria could heal her master of the dreaded disease of leprosy. Believing the girl's words, Naaman went to Israel. When the king of Israel sent Naaman to the prophet Elisha, Elisha told his servant to tell Naaman to dip seven times in the Jordan River and he would be healed. But Naaman became very angry and complained that he could have washed in rivers in Syria if that would have cured him. Finally, Naaman's servants convinced him to do what the prophet had instructed. Seven times Naaman dipped himself in the Jordan River, and when he came up the seventh time, he was completely cured (2 Kings 5).

Too often we look at life the same way Naaman did. We seek satisfaction in life's activities without considering the purpose behind them. It wasn't the river that healed Naaman, but his obedience to God's purpose through the words of the prophet Elisha. The river was powerless. God's word is all-powerful. When He determines a purpose for our lives, we will find fulfillment only when we are walking toward the end He has set.

God wants us to know His plans and purposes for our lives because He knows that apart from them we cannot know hope, peace and joy. In all things, purpose is the key to fulfillment because it establishes the foundation on which all life must be built.

❖ **PRINCIPLES** ❖

1. God does everything *with* and *for* a purpose.

2. Everything serves a purpose.

3. Unknown purpose always wastes time and gives the possibility of danger.

4. Abuse and misuse occur when purpose isn't known.

5. A person or thing apart from its creator cannot know its purpose.

6. If you want to know the purpose of a product, you must ask the manufacturer or his authorized representative.

7. Purpose reveals the reasons behind life's experiences and demands, supplies a vision for the future and gives life significance and meaning.

CHAPTER FOUR

The Priority of Purpose

Purpose precedes creation.

Every child is delighted by a tour through a car factory or a book printer. With wide-eyed wonder they look at the finished product then go back to the beginning to see all the steps that went into the making of that car or book. As they walk through the factory and listen to the guide describe the various processes, they often ask questions like, "What does this do?" "Why is she doing that?" Their questions hint at the truth that the *why* is more important than the *what*. Knowing what the various parts of a product are is useless unless you understand why they were designed that way and how they are supposed to fit together.

Purpose Determines Function, Which Necessitates Design

If I went to a contractor and asked him to construct a building for me, his first question would be, "What is your purpose for this building?" That would be the underlying concern for the whole project: Why do I want this building to exist and what do I want it to accomplish? Thus, establishing the purpose for the building is the first priority.

After that is settled, the contractor would probably say to me: "Let me see your plans. I need to see how your architect designed the building." As he looked over the plans, the contractor would consider whether they revealed a design that would allow the building to function in a manner that would meet the determined purpose.

Let's say, for example, that I wanted the contractor to erect a building that could be used for providing medical care. The building must, therefore, meet the needs of doctors, nurses, X-ray and lab technicians, patients, and so on, and the design must facilitate that performance. Thus, the purpose for the building determines its function, and the function necessitates design. If the building is to function as a doctor's office, its design will be quite different than that of a hospital.

Let's consider another example. If my wife wants to sew a dress (purpose), she will design the dress to meet her needs for either summer or winter wear (function). She might make a dress for winter out of heavy material and style it with a snug fit, a high neck, long sleeves and fur trim. A summer dress, on the other hand, might be cut from a lightweight material and fashioned with a loose fit, a low neckline, short sleeves, and lace or net trim. The winter dress, whose function is to keep her warm, would reveal that in its design. Likewise, the summer dress would be styled to keep her cool and comfortable during hot weather. In essence, *what* you are and *how* you are was predetermined by *why* you are. Your design is perfect for your purpose.

Your design is perfect for your purpose.

Purpose Produces Design, and Design Predicts Potential

If I'm going to create something that will fly, I must first decide that the object's purpose is to fly. Then I have to determine what function and design will allow the object to accomplish that expectation. In other words, I will put into the kite, the helicopter or the airplane the ability to do what I am asking it to do. My design will include whatever is needed for the object to fly. Because I intended for the object to fly and I built into it the ability to fly, the object can fly. Therefore, purpose produces design and design predicts potential. From looking at an object's design you can predict what it is capable of doing.

To back up a step, purpose is also an indication of potential. *If you know the intended purpose for an object, you also know what it can do.* The minute you know that the kite was created to fly, you know that it can fly. Therefore, whatever you were born to do—whatever God purposed for your life—you are equipped with all the ability, talents, gifts, capacities and potential you need to fulfill it. You can do all things (purpose) through Christ, who supplies the ability.

Purpose Determines Nature

When someone creates something, they create it in such a way as to fulfill its purpose. They build into it the essence of what makes the thing unique, because what they do to create it becomes its nature. In essence, the purpose of a thing determines its nature.

The word *nature,* as defined by Webster, means "the particular combination of qualities belonging to a person, animal, thing or class by birth, origin or construction." It is that of which something is naturally composed. I want to emphasize "naturally."

When God creates something, He puts into it the ability to fulfill its function. Birds were created to fly, so their wings and the shape of their bodies make the air their natural environment. Oh, they may sit on the ground or in trees, and they may love your cages, bird houses and bird baths, but they don't really prefer to be there. Birds are happiest when they are flying. Just watch a hawk soaring above the trees or a barn swallow diving after insects. They love to fly because God created them to fly. That is both their purpose and their nature. *Nature is inherent in purpose.*

Or consider fish. Their bodies are constructed to glide through the sea and to withstand water pressure that would harm other creatures. If man wants to build a ship, he must learn from the design of fish what will and will not withstand the pounding of the ocean. He must also consider the nature of ducks that allows them to glide on the top of the water. Thus, a boat must naturally include the abilities to float and to withstand water pressure.

The nature of something is a powerful clue to its purpose and potential. Take a bulldozer. One day as I sat and watched a bulldozer working close to our house, the thought came to me that I could tell its purpose just by looking at its nature. The shovel on a bulldozer is not used to scoop out ice cream nor was it intended to move furniture around your house. The design tells you that very quickly. The size of the scoop is far too big for any ice cream container and the teeth that dig into the earth would quickly ruin furniture.

The nature of something is a powerful clue to its purpose and potential.

When God created you, He built into you all the natural necessities for performing and fulfilling your purposed assignment. Everyone possesses natural inherent traits that are required for their purpose. In essence, you are the *way* you are because of *why* you are.

Purpose Coincides with Natural Talents and Abilities

The purpose of a thing, which is revealed in its design and nature, is always accompanied by certain innate abilities. They are there naturally. Owls naturally have the ability to see in the dark because God created them to gather their food at night and to sleep during the day. Spiders have the ability to spin webs because that's how they snare their food. Woodpeckers have strong, sharply pointed bills for digging into tree trunks and branches for wood-boring insects. *Purpose never requires something that natural abilities do not provide for.*

When I was thirteen years old, I submitted my life to God and made a conscious, quality decision to discover personal peace. I was so happy to be a Christian and I experienced great excitement. One day my pastor said to me, "Great, praise the Lord. That's a good thing to do. But don't stop there. You have to find *God's will* for your life." So I went on this long search looking for *God's will*. Well, after one year passed without my finding that will, and then a second year as well, I became discouraged. In fact, I was so discouraged that I just stopped looking. Part of the problem was that I feared God's will would be the opposite of what I liked to do or wanted to be. So there I was praying, "Oh, God, show me Your will. I hope it's what I want to do, Lord, but show it to me anyhow."

There's a problem with that prayer because it assumes something that isn't true. Just as a manufacturer does not demand or expect anything from his product that he did not design it to do, God never requires anything of His creations that He didn't already build into them. What they naturally are is what He asks. He requires butterflies to fly because that's their nature. He demands that caterpillars crawl because He designed them to crawl. Apple trees are obligated to produce apples because He placed the seeds within them to do just that.

> **God never requires anything of His creations that He didn't already build into them.**

Consider God's creation of Lucifer. His purpose for creating this being was that he should be responsible for worship in Heaven. The Scriptures teach that he was created as beautiful as the morning star, wise and elegant. But most importantly, his very being was created with organ pipes built into it because of his purpose. This principle is true for all created things and manufactured products.

Perhaps you have a friend who is really into music. Everything in his life in some way reveals his love for music. There's an organ in the living room, a piano in the dining room, a harpsichord in the family room, a CD player in the kitchen and a huge stereo in the bedroom. Every room in the house in some way reflects his love for music because his whole life is music. Can you imagine God calling that man to be a butcher or a factory worker? That would be a prescription for frustration.

God puts into everything the potential and the nature for its purpose. Purpose, therefore, is accompanied by natural abilities. *You are naturally like what you are supposed to do.* If He didn't build it into you, He won't ask you to do it, because purpose is always accompanied by the innate qualities and characteristics it requires. You have what you need to be who you are. What you love and desire to do naturally is usually what you were born to do. *Purpose allows you to be yourself. The discovery of purpose is the discovery of you.*

You have what you need to be who you are.

Purpose Determines Demand, and Demand Dictates Potential

You can make a demand on something if you know the purpose for its existence. Let's use the example of a tape recorder. If you purchase a stereo component that contains a piece of equipment that the instruction booklet calls a cassette tape player, you can put a tape in the indicated slot, push the play button and expect the stereo to produce music. When you press "play," you are making a demand on the equipment because the manufacturer told you that the equipment will replay a prerecorded tape. In other words, the purpose predicted the demand you could make on the product.

Consider also the difference in expectation you would have of an 18-wheeler tractor trailer and a 2-door sports car. Because their purposes differ, your expectations and demands on them would also be different.

If God tells you why you were born, He is also telling you what's inside you. If God says, "I gave you birth to produce beautiful music to express the beauty and harmony of My nature and so win scores of people to Me before you die," I'm telling you, friend, there is enough music in you to reach a million people. When God told Moses to free His people, He was also telling him, "The ability to perform what I've required of you is inside you. Go do it, because you can." Moses had a problem with that and he started arguing with God.

Then the Lord said to him, "What is that in your hand?"

"A staff," he [Moses] replied.

The Lord said, "Throw it on the ground."

Moses threw it on the ground and it became a snake, and he ran from it. Then the Lord said to him, "Reach out your hand and take it by the tail." So Moses reached out and took hold of the snake and it turned back into a staff in his hand (Exodus 4:2-4).

As Moses continued to argue with God, God first made Moses' hand leprous, then He restored it. Finally, when Moses complained that he was not eloquent of speech, God asked him:

Who gave man his mouth? Who makes him deaf or mute? Who gives him sight or makes him blind? Is it not I, the Lord? Now go; I will help you speak and will teach you what to say (Exodus 4:11-12).

In other words, God is saying, "Who made this product, and who designed this equipment?" How can the pot say to the potter, "Why did you make me thus?"

After God, in anger, finally agreed to send Aaron with him as his spokesman, Moses stopped resisting the assignment. He asked his father-in-law Jethro for permission to return to Egypt. Throughout his encounter with the Pharoah of Egypt, Moses learned what God had built into him before his birth. As he discovered the purpose for his existence, he also found out that God provided both the potential and the provisions to meet every assignment.

The same is true in your life. *Your purpose determines your potential, which determines the demands made on you by the One who made you.* Knowing your purpose is the key to using your potential, because once you discover your purpose in life you can also learn how much potential God stored inside you to meet the demands He would make on you. *If you don't know your purpose, you will probably live below your potential. Potential is equal to purpose.*

> **Potential is equal to purpose.**

Provisions Go With the Assignment

A manufacturer not only creates something for a purpose, he also provides the potential to fulfill that purpose. Purpose has in it the potential to fulfill itself. In essence, if you make a lawn mower, you will put into the mower the potential to cut grass.

It's important to know the purpose for your life because your assignment and your provisions are related to that purpose. Whenever God gives you an assignment, He also is responsible for the provisions for that assignment. *What God calls for He provides for.* He will never call you to do anything without providing the resources to accomplish that task. This does not mean that God will provide for every plan you undertake, because He is not obligated to pay for something He didn't buy. If your plans are not in tune with His purpose, you may encounter problems completing everything you've undertaken.

Many folks are doing work for God that God didn't ask them to do, and they are asking Him to pay the bill. God doesn't work that way. He provides for His purposes, not our plans. The Church, in particular, is guilty of this error.

Remember, many are the plans in a man's heart, but the Lord's purpose prevails.

> **God provides for His purposes, not our plans.**

Jesus told His disciples after Peter announced that He was the Christ:

> **Blessed are you, Simon son of Jonah, for this was not revealed to you by man, but by My Father in heaven. And I tell you that you are Peter, and on this rock I will build My church, and the gates of Hades [or hell] will not overcome it** (Matthew 16:17-18).

Ecclesia, the Greek word for *church*, means "called out ones." This definition says nothing about buildings or bells or steeples or benches or pews or organs. *Ecclessia* is people. Thus, this verse means: Upon this rock I will build My people—My called out ones—and they will be so powerful that hell itself will not control them.

Wow! That's power. But where is it? Too often the Church is everything but powerful because we are asking God to bless plans that He didn't make. God's intention for the Church was not to have church services and children's church and choirs and women's meetings. God wants us to be His "called out ones" to reveal His "manifold wisdom" (Ephesians 3:10). The Greek word *popupoikilos* is used here to describe God's wisdom. It literally means "many-colored." What a description for God's wisdom. It can take whatever form it needs to take to meet the challenges that face His Church.

Too often the Church is so busy with her own plans that she fails to expose God's wisdom in sending Jesus Christ into the world. Many people are so busy building their ministries, their buildings, their programs and their projects, that they are not fulfilling their purpose. Through Christ, sin and death and evil are defeated forever.

If the devil is winning in our lives, our communities or our countries, it is because the Church is not doing her job. She is not fulfilling her purpose. When we expose God, He provides the resources to continue our efforts. It is as though He says to us, "Come on, Church, show them something else. Show them what I am really like."

Excellence is looking like God. It is showing the qualities and the essence of the epitome of God. It is not doing a mediocre job with half-hearted enthusiasm. God asks the Church to be holy because He is holy, and His sons and daughters came out of Him. He requires those who carry His name to love their enemies because He is love, and He put that love in them when He made them. He demands that His children turn the other cheek when someone misuses them because His Son, Jesus, who faithfully exposed the Father's nature, turned the other cheek to purchase our salvation, and we are heirs of God with Christ. Until the Church takes seriously her calling to expose the totality of God's love, grace and power, she will continue to struggle, because she is asking God to provide for plans that are not His.

God will not ask His "called out ones" to do something that He has not provided for. The demands He places on His people reveal the potential He placed within them before their birth. With each and every demand always come the provisions to accomplish the task. He is not in agreement with the Church when she tells Him what she cannot do. God's sons and daughters are covered so long as they discover His purpose and walk in it.

> **God's sons and daughters are covered so long as they discover His purpose and walk in it.**

Oh, there may be some roadblocks along the way, but God will always provide a window when the door slams shut. He needs some people who will be obedient long enough to see the provisions for the assignments He gives. Purpose doesn't make those tasks easy, it makes them possible. In essence, every manufacturer provides genuine parts and services for his product. God does the same for you according to His purpose.

Promises Are Related to Purpose

The protection, security, credibility and true value of a product is not how much it cost you, but the stability and security of the manufacturer. The manufacturer's warranty is only as good as the strength of the parent company. It doesn't matter what the company promises when you buy the product, if the company is no longer around to make good that promise, the promise is null, void and useless. So, the most important thing is not the promise but the promiser.

Perhaps you bought a car that is no longer made. Not only has the company discontinued the car model, they have also stopped making parts. Now the only place you can find replacement parts for your car is the junk yard. *Warranties mean nothing when the company can no longer keep its promises.*

Promises, warranties and guarantees are made to maintain, sustain and produce the purpose of the product. When a company makes a warranty, they are not going to first check out your environment, your present conditions or what's happening in your state. Their only concern is that you abide by the terms in the warranty. Any other conditions do not affect how the manufacturer determines the contents of the warranty and the conditions under which it will be applied.

Guarantees are made from the perspective of the manufacturer, not the consumer. If it's raining or a hurricane is coming or the dog just got killed or you just lost your job, the warranty is still good as long as the terms specified within it are met. The manufacturer doesn't care what else is happening in your life. If you meet the conditions of the warranty, he'll send the part. Your environment is not part of his considerations.

God's promises to us are the same way. Their value is based on the stability and credibility of God. Unlike many manufacturers, God will never go out of business. He will keep His promises forever because they are made to maintain, sustain and produce His purposes for our individual lives and for humanity in general. His promises cannot fail because His purposes always prevail.

God's promises are based on His stability and credibility.

Like the warranties of human manufacturers, *God's promises are not dependent on our environment.* The conditions in our lives do not affect His ability to keep them. God is more concerned about our relationship with Him and our faithfulness in meeting His demands than the conditions around us that change our perspective on His promises. He wants us to trust His willingness and ability to keep His promises no matter what is going on in our lives. *We do not need to help God meet His obligations.*

As we mentioned in a previous chapter, Abraham and Sarah learned this when Sarah became impatient because twenty-five years had passed since God had promised them a son and she still was not a mother. God did not accept Sarah's attempt to assist Him by giving her maid Hagar to Abraham so they might have a son through her. When Hagar's son Ishmael was born, God said that Ishmael was not the son of promise because that child was to be born through Sarah.

> [Abraham's] **son by the slave woman was born in the ordinary way; but his son by the free woman was born as the result of a promise** (Galatians 4:23).

Your plans do not and cannot change God's purposes any more than Sarah's plans did. God will stick with His warranty even if you come up with a plan that looks nice. He's stuck with His promise, and His promise is related to His purpose. Even though Sarah laughed and tried to substitute her plan for God's, she still received the son of promise.

Your plans do not and cannot change God's purposes.

No matter how much you would like God to support you in your plans to help Him keep His promises, God will only support His purpose. *God is totally obligated to support you if you are in His purposes,* but if you are outside them, forget it. *His promises are more powerful than your plans.* Sarah's plan was not part of God's purpose, so He didn't support it. His promises go with His purpose, because all warranties are related to the prior purpose of the manufacturer.

So we see that purpose always precedes and influences the function, design, potential, nature and innate abilities of a product. Purpose also predetermines the demands and the assignments the creator asks of a product and the provisions he supplies to meet those requirements. Finally, purpose is a priority to promises because promises are made to enable the product to fulfill the creator's original intent.

What God calls for He provides for.

❖ PRINCIPLES ❖

1. *What* you are and *how* you are was predetermined by *why* you are.

2. Your ability to fulfill your purpose and your potential is built into your function and design.

3. Your design gives clues to your purpose and your potential.

4. You are equipped with everything you need to fulfill your purpose.

5. God's assignments reveal your abilities and your capabilities.

6. God provides both the potential and the provisions to meet every assignment.

7. Knowing your purpose is the key to using your potential.

8. Provisions are made to maintain, sustain and produce God's purpose for your life.

CHAPTER FIVE

Purpose and Time

**Life without purpose
is time without meaning.**

Have you ever sat in an airport or a train station and watched the people moving through the building? Some walk slowly and casually. Others stride hurriedly and intently, perhaps sprinting or running. The difference in pace is often related to time. Some are early. Others are late. Each is there for a purpose, either future or imminent.

Time is an important part of our lives. It gives order to our days and allows us to set schedules. But schedules in and of themselves are worthless unless we have a purpose behind the schedule. It is useless to keep track of time if there is no end toward which we are moving.

**It is useless to keep track of time
if there is no end toward which we are moving.**

A Time for Everything

The Book of Ecclesiastes presents an important perspective on time. I think it is helpful to read this Scripture in several translations:

> **There is a time for everything, and a season for every activity under heaven** (Ecclesiastes 3:1).
>
> **To everything there is a season, a time for every purpose under heaven** (NKJV).
>
> **Everything that happens in this world happens at the time God chooses** (GN).
>
> **There is a right time for everything. And everything on earth will happen at the right time** (ETRV).

This verse suggests that the time at which something happens is significant. What may be helpful and right at one time is wrong at another. The truth of this observation is evident throughout our lives.

Parents rejoice when a happily-married daughter announces that she is expecting her first child. The pregnancy is usually a happy period as the parents and the grandparents prepare to welcome the new child. When the mother-to-be is a sixteen-year-old girl, however, the coming birth is often viewed quite differently. The explanation for the difference lies in the matter of timing.

Or consider the contrast between the events surrounding the birth of a full-term baby and a premature child. The full-term child is usually given to the mother only minutes after birth, but a premature child is quickly whisked to the nursery and placed in an incubator. The first days of the fully-developed child are spent in the arms of his parents and in a bassinet beside the mother's bed, while the child who is born early is confined to a neonatal nursery hooked to an IV, a respirator and a heart monitor. Again, the reason behind the differences are related to time.

Defining Time

Webster defines time as "the system of those sequential relations that any event has to any other, as past, present, or future" or "a system or method of measuring or reckoning the passage of time." Thus, we establish the time of something in terms of previous and future events, and we measure the passage of time in terms of seconds, minutes, hours, days, weeks, years and centuries. Birth, growth, aging and death are also part of our vocabulary related to time.

Time is such an important part of our concept of life that many of our conversations center around it: How old are you? When did you move to this community? How long have you worked at this job? When were you married? How soon will you finish this assignment?

Such questions, however, are never God's questions. He is not interested in how old you are. Neither is He concerned with how many years you have performed a particular job. In fact, He may be saddened by the time it has taken you to complete a particular task or learn a new truth.

An Eternal Perspective

Time can also be defined as the "duration regarded as belonging to the present life as distinct from the life to come or from eternity." This is the perspective from which God operates because He is a God of purpose, and every purpose has a time. The minute something drops into the realm of this planet—into the physical, material world—it picks up time. When it leaves here, time is canceled. Eternity is duration without measure.

Or to say it another way, time is a temporary interruption in eternity. Eternity has neither a beginning nor an end, for it is outside time. Time, on the other hand, starts the minute we are born and ends when we die. It is but a brief part of our existence.

> **Time is a temporary interruption in eternity.**

God, who is eternal, therefore exists outside time. He is not against time, for He is its Creator and He pronounced everything that He created to be very good (Genesis 1:31). God is simply outside time even though He works with people who are in time.

This difference often makes us think that God is very slow in responding to our needs. We think He is late in coming to our aid, which causes us to question whether God really cares about us. The prophet Isaiah speaks to the differences between our perspective on time and God's:

> **"For My thoughts are not your thoughts, neither are your ways My ways," declares the Lord. "As the heavens are higher than the earth, so are My ways higher than your ways and My thoughts than your thoughts. ...My word that goes out from My mouth: It will not return to Me empty, but will accomplish what I desire and achieve the purpose for which I sent it"** (Isaiah 55:8-9,11).

This difference in perspective is related to purpose. God, who sees the end from the beginning, sets our course in accordance with His overall purpose, not our immediate needs. His timing is always better than ours because He sees our whole lives and how they fit into His entire purpose for ourselves and others. Could we but understand His purposes when we want something today or yesterday, He would say to us, "If I come now, it won't be the best. I'm waiting to give you the best I have." That doesn't mean He is unconcerned for us. In reality, His concern keeps Him from giving us what we want. Many times God comes late and it is the right time.

The Purpose of Time

When God created us in time, He set a certain time for the height of our maturity. After that beauty declines, we are ready to move into eternity. This is possible because time is not our permanent home. God placed us within time but made us to be eternal beings:

> **He has made everything beautiful in its time. He has also set eternity in the hearts of men; yet they cannot fathom what God has done from beginning to end** (Ecclesiastes 3:11).

The word *beauty* has to do with maturation, fulfillment and perfection. In other words, God creates everything with a purpose and gives every purpose a time that allows it to progress to perfection. He makes everything beautiful in the time He gives it.

God makes everything beautiful in the time He gives it.

Consider, for a moment, a rose. In the spring before the rose bush blooms, it is ugly. Thorns cover the stems and tiny, hard green things stick out among the leaves. After a few weeks, these little green things slowly begin to open until you can see the color of the petals. Then the bud begins to open and the individual petals become visible. Still, the rose is not what it yet can be. It has not reached the height of its beauty. There comes a point when the fully opened rose reaches perfection. It can be no more beautiful.

Its shape and color are in perfect harmony. After perfection is reached, death and decay set in. The flowers whither and brown until the petals fall from the bush. It fulfills its purpose and then naturally dies. Nothing should die until its purpose is fulfilled.

The Book of Ecclesiastes says that there is a time for every purpose under Heaven (Ecclesiastes 3:1), thus time is always given for a purpose. It is never intended to be idle and empty. In the early spring as new shoots are coming up in the garden, the richness of harvest is but a dream or an expectation. Time must do its work. As the summer progresses, the plants grow and blossom. Fruit begins to cover the plants and the vines. By midsummer the harvest has begun. Peas, beans and tomatoes have been picked and enjoyed. But the time of harvest is not complete. Pumpkins and sweet potatoes have not yet matured. Cantaloupe and watermelon still cling to the vine. The completeness of the garden's purpose has not yet been reached.

God always makes things come to maturity within His specified time. He has built into all creation the ability to find completeness, fulfillment, perfection and beauty before its time is past. This is as true for men and women as for any plant within the garden.

God created you for a specific purpose and gave you the exact amount of time required to fulfill your purpose. In essence, your length of physical life is determined by your purpose.

God created you for a specific purpose and gave you the exact amount of time required to fulfill your purpose.

Time and Your Purpose

God's creation of man reveals that He desired a time-conscious being with an eternity perspective. You were born and created for a purpose in God's plan, and you were given a time to fulfill that purpose. According to the Scriptures, *there is a time to every purpose* (Ecclesiastes 3:1). Because we live in time, we measure life in increments of seconds, minutes, hours, days, months, years, etc. But how does God measure and judge the success of your life? To answer this we must consider that God never intended for us to die.

God's original purpose and His future plans call for us to live forever. Therefore, length of years is not the measure of life for God. Your age does not impress Him. There are many who believe that old age is a sign of God's favor and approval. If this is true, then how do you account for the millions of individuals in countries like Siberia, Prussia and Rumania, and perhaps even in your city, who live beyond one hundred years of age and have no commitment to God? Their life styles incorporate behaviors that are considered to be ungodly. It is evident that God measures the success, effectiveness and value of your life on earth in terms of purpose.

God's question is never "How many years have you lived?" or "How old are you?" but rather "What have you done?" In essence, life is not measured by duration but by donation. From God's perspective, "Well done" is more important than "Long lived."

Jesus understood the important relationship between time and the completion of purpose. Again and again He instructed people not to move faster in their expectations of Him than God's perfect timing allowed. This awareness of God's purpose for His life as it related to His time on earth is particularly evident in John's record of the wedding at Cana.

> On the third day a wedding took place at Cana in Galilee. Jesus' mother was there, and Jesus and His disciples had also been invited to the wedding. When the wine was gone, Jesus' mother said to Him, "They have no more wine."
>
> "Dear woman, why do you involve Me?" Jesus replied. "My time has not yet come" (John 2:1-4).

Jesus also displayed this consciousness of time and purpose on many other occasions. In the twelth chapter of the Gospel of John He says,

> The hour has come for the Son of Man to be glorified. ... Now My heart is troubled, and what shall I say? "Father, save Me from this hour"? No, it was for this very reason that I came to this hour. Father, glorify Your name! (John 12:23,27)

He further expresses the relationship of time and timing to purpose in the seventh chapter of John:

> Jesus' brothers said to Him, "You ought to leave here and go to Judea, so that Your disciples may see the miracles You do. No one who wants to become a public figure acts in secret. Since You are doing these things, show Yourself to the world." For even His own brothers did not believe in Him. Therefore Jesus told them, "The right time for Me has not yet come; for you any time is right" (John 7:3-6).

Here Jesus' disciples attempted to influence Him to go public and declare His power and position. But Jesus refused and stated that there was *a right time* for every purpose of God and *a right timing* for it to be released in its fullness. He further informed them that they had no awareness of the purpose and the proper use of time for their own lives.

Therefore, it is vital for you to capture and maximize the time of your life. To do this, you must discover your purpose for life and get busy with your assignment. Every day should be used to account for the fulfillment of God's dream in your heart. What have you done with the last year, month or day that you've lived? What can you show to justify that time?

Time was given to you to fulfill your purpose in this life. Don't be like Methuselah, of whom it is recorded that he lived 969 years and then died. That is all we know of his life. What a tragedy! I admonish you to find your purpose and give time meaning. As the apostle Paul exhorts: "See then that you walk circumspectly, not as fools but as wise, redeeming the time, because the days are evil" (Ephesians 5:15-16 NKJV).

Throughout His ministry, glimpses of Jesus' true nature and glory were visible. He healed the sick (John 4:43-53, among many), multiplied loaves of bread and fish to feed large crowds (John 6:1-15), walked on the Sea of Galilee (John 6:16-20), and brought sinful people to repentance (John 4:1-42).

As the time for His crucifixion drew near, Jesus acknowledged that His time had come:

> **Father, the time has come. Glorify Your Son, that Your Son may glorify You. For You granted Him authority over all people that He might give eternal life to all those You have given Him. Now this is eternal life: that they may know You, the only true God, and Jesus Christ, whom You have sent. I have brought You glory on earth by completing the work You gave Me to do. And now, Father, glorify Me in Your presence with the glory I had with You before the world began (John 17:1-5).**

Time is always given for the completion of purpose. Whenever time is used for things that do not work toward the given purpose, it is wasted and the opportunity to reach perfection is delayed or lost.

> **Time is always given for the completion of purpose.**

Jesus came to reconnect us with our God-given purpose and the importance of using time to complete that purpose. His goal was not Calvary but the resurrection, so He could redirect our living from time to eternity.

God has given you an assignment that is so awesome it will take you this life and the life to come to complete it. He invites you to live by faith, moving with Him beyond the limitations of what you can see, hear and feel at any given moment, so your perspective can move from living for today alone to looking toward eternity.

There's eternity in your heart because God placed it there. Knowing your purpose and the time associated with it will allow you to be effective and productive in your living, using the time He gives you for the purpose for which He gave it. The proper use of time is always dependent on the priority of purpose because time is an interruption in eternity that allows you to fulfill what you were sent here to do.

He who has time to burn will never give the world much light. Killing time is not murder, it's suicide.

Teach us to number our days aright, that we may gain a heart of wisdom.

Psalm 90:12

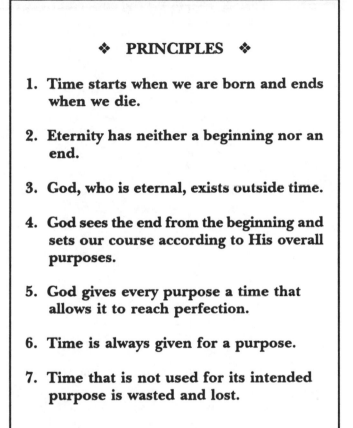

❖ **PRINCIPLES** ❖

1. Time starts when we are born and ends when we die.

2. Eternity has neither a beginning nor an end.

3. God, who is eternal, exists outside time.

4. God sees the end from the beginning and sets our course according to His overall purposes.

5. God gives every purpose a time that allows it to reach perfection.

6. Time is always given for a purpose.

7. Time that is not used for its intended purpose is wasted and lost.

❖ NOTES ❖

CHAPTER SIX

Purpose and Position

**Status without purpose
is position without authority.**

One afternoon a mother took her son to the local elementary school for soccer practice. She returned an hour and a half later to find an angry, tearful child. When she asked him what was wrong, he said, "My practice wasn't here today. It was at the park. We must have read the schedule wrong. So, I had to sit and watch the other teams practice. It was so boring! Now I'm afraid my coach won't let me play in the game on Saturday because I missed practice."

Most of us have had the experience of being at the wrong place. We've waited at one entrance to the store while our friends were looking for us at another. Or we've waited at a customer service desk to exchange a purchase, only to find that we had to go to the department where the purchase was made. Such experiences are disturbing because we cannot achieve what we set out to do.

Such frustration is minor compared to the turmoil created by our competition to excel and reach a position of prestige and honor. This desire to get ahead is a compelling passion in our world. Every person has been bitten by this aspiration to rise in status. We are preoccupied with the status quo and we seek to gain status symbols. We want the best for ourselves with little or no concern for those we climb over in our pursuit for a position of power.

> **The desire to get ahead is a compelling passion in our world.**

The desire for status is an age-old problem. From the time we are very young, we learn to do the things that enhance our status and bring us prominence and prestige. Even Jesus' disciples were not free from the suffocating grip of this ambition.

Who Is the Greatest?

The Gospel of Mark describes the status seeking of James and John, two of Jesus' closest disciples. As the time for Jesus' death drew near and He spoke to His disciples of His impending arrest, James and John, the sons of Zebedee, asked Jesus for a favor: "Let one of us sit at Your right and the other at Your left in Your glory" (Mark 10:37). Jesus cautioned them that they did not know what they were requesting and asked whether they could endure what He would need to endure. When they assured Him they could, He agreed that they would share His suffering but that the places beside Him in glory were not His to grant.

When the other ten disciples heard about the request James and John had made of Jesus, they became angry and resentful. Not too many days before they had been arguing on the road about who was the greatest. This desire of James and John undoubtedly caused the emotions generated by that discussion to resurface.

On that occasion Jesus had taught them that he who wants to be first "must be the very last, and the servant of all" (Mark 9:35). Now He taught them that "whoever wants to be first must be the slave of all" and reminded them that He had "not come to be served, but to serve, and to give His life as a ransom for many" (Mark 10:43-45).

Defining Status

Status literally means "the state of us." Webster defines it as a "condition or position with regard to the law." Thus, status is position. Webster also describes status as "the position of an individual in relation to another"—showing that status has to do with rank—and "the state or condition of affairs." Status is not just a random ordering of things, but a careful positioning that reveals the relationships between people or the parts of a whole.

The Scriptures reveal that God takes very seriously this issue of position. He ordained in creation that everything in life has a purpose and a relationship to everything else within God's universe. Or to say it another way, *the principle of status states that everything has a purpose, which determines its status in relationship to everything else.* God also consistently reveals in His Word that position is given, not for personal gain, but for the good of all.

The Responsibility of Status

When I went to junior high school, I wanted to become an A student because A students are respected and appreciated. Everybody speaks to you and the teachers love you. In other words, my purpose for trying to attain the A student status had nothing to do with a desire to help others. I was out to grab all I could for myself.

Similar things happen in the workplace. Perhaps you are part of an office where fake games are played. Somebody's always making the coffee, vacuuming the floor or making copies. Now all these are necessary tasks, but the motive behind the action is of primary importance. Are these things being done as a service to others or are they a way to gain special recognition and advancement?

The apostle Paul warns against the destruction and futility of seeking position for personal gain.

> ...Do not think of yourself more highly than you ought, but rather think of yourself with sober judgment, in accordance with the measure of faith God has given you. Just as each of us has one body with many members, and these members do not all have same function, so in Christ we who are many form one body, and each members belongs to all the others (Romans 12:3-5).

> ...I urge you to live a life worthy of the calling you have received. Be completely humble and gentle; be patient, bearing with one another in love. Make every effort to keep the unity of the Spirit through the bond of peace. There is one body and one Spirit—just as you were called to one hope when you were called—one Lord, one faith, one baptism; one God and Father of all, who is over all and through all and in all (Ephesians 4:1-6).

This humility and consideration for others occurs most easily when each part of the body knows and values its position as well as the positions of others.

> It was He [Christ] who gave some to be apostles, some to be prophets, some to be evangelists, and some to be pastors and teachers, to prepare God's people for works of service, so that the body of Christ may be built up until we all reach unity in the faith and in the knowledge of the Son of God and become mature, attaining to the whole measure of the fullness of Christ (Ephesians 4:11-13).

We see that position is not given to show the value of one person or part of the body over another. Thus, visible position does not equal greater value. Each part is to do his task to the best of his ability to benefit the whole. Those in leadership receive that status to strengthen everyone.

Visible position does not equal greater value.

The Importance of Position

This importance of position is evident throughout life. Let's use the example of a telephone to illustrate this truth.

A telephone has many parts, some visible and some invisible. Among the visible parts are the receiver, the mouthpiece, the cord between the wall jack and the phone, the cord between the handset and the base unit, the buttons or disk for dialing, and the base unit of the phone. Internally there may be wires, a ringer, a battery, an amplifier (if it a speaker phone) and so on.

If the ringer decides it no longer wants to be a ringer but prefers to be the base unit because it is highly visible, the caller would never reach his party because the phone would not audibly ring. Or if the cord between the handset and the base unit tries to act like the buttons or the disk for dialing, the phone would ring but the caller would not be able to communicate with the person he called because the receiver and the mouthpiece would not be connected to the body of the phone.

Like the parts of a phone, each person God creates has a specific place within the overall scheme of His plan for the world. Character, nature, gifts and position are specially designed to fulfill whatever task God purposed for each individual. Frustration results whenever we try to fulfill a position that we are not designed to occupy, because failure to accomplish our God-given tasks is disobedience.

Just Because It's Good Doesn't Mean It's Right

The key to obedience is understanding status. Many people are disobedient and don't know it. They are doing good things that are not the right things because they are out of position. God's attitude toward obedience says that to almost obey, to obey too soon, to obey too late, to obey in the wrong place and to obey with the wrong person are all disobedience. The prophet Samuel expressed this truth after God took His anointing from King Saul, who had desired to worship God with offerings obtained through disobedience. Saul wanted to do a good thing that was not right.

> **The Lord said to Samuel, "How long will you mourn for Saul, since I have rejected him as king over Israel? Fill your horn with oil and be on your way; I am sending you to Jesse of Bethlehem. I have chosen one of his sons to be king"** (1 Samuel 16:1).

Many people are disobedient and don't know it.

God also had to speak to Moses about trying to do more than his God-given task. God accomplished this through Jethro, Moses' father-in-law.

> **What is this you are doing for the people? Why do you alone sit as judge, while all these people stand around you from morning till evening? ...What you are doing is not good. You and these people who come to you will only wear yourselves out. The work is too heavy for you; you cannot handle it alone. ... You must be the people's representative before God...but select capable men from all the people...[and] have them serve as judges for the people...** (Exodus 18:14,17-18,19,21,22)

There will never be a lack of need in this world. If you are driven to meet everyone's needs, you will not be able to meet even those needs that God wants you to meet. Doing the right thing, and not just the good thing, requires that you find your God-given purpose and position and stay there. Obedience doesn't consist of following the prescribed do's and don'ts. It involves doing the right thing in the right place at the right time. When you stray from that place, you hurt yourself and others, because *violation of status always causes chaos and destruction.*

> **Obedience is doing the right thing in the right place at the right time.**

The Violation of Status

The major dilemmas that plague our world are related to a violation of position. This predicament goes back to the first human beings when Adam and Eve got out of position. No longer content to be creatures, they sought to take the place of God.

Think for a moment what would happen if the members of a basketball team became dissatisfied with their positions and decided to take someone else's place. No one would know who was going to defend against baskets, who was going up for rebounds and who was going to take the ball down the floor to score. Teamwork would be impossible with everyone out of position, and each player would constantly be jostling the members of his own team. Such a lack of cooperation would soon destroy the team.

The jealousy and envy behind such dissatisfaction became evident in the lives of Miriam and Aaron, Moses' brother and sister, so that they began to talk against him:

"Has the Lord spoken only through Moses? ... Hasn't He also spoken through us?" (Numbers 12:2) When the Lord heard this, He told Moses, Miriam and Aaron go out to the Tent of Meeting, where He met them in a pillar of cloud.

> He [God] stood at the entrance to the Tent and summoned Aaron and Miriam. When both of them stepped forward, He said: "Listen to My words: When a prophet of the Lord is among you, I reveal Myself to him in visions, I speak to him in dreams. But this is not true of My servant Moses; he is faithful in all My house. With him I speak face to face, clearly and not in riddles; he sees the form of the Lord. Why then were you not afraid to speak against My servant Moses?" (Numbers 12:5-8)

The Lord had to reprimand Miriam and Aaron because they were out of position. So great was His anger that Miriam had leprosy when the cloud of the Lord lifted. When Aaron pleaded with Moses not to hold their foolishness against them, Moses prayed to the Lord for her healing. God answered his prayer, but He required that Miriam remain a leper for seven days.

Our position or status in life is determined by our purpose. Every item in a car engine is different, vital and unique, but it is located in the engine based on the purpose it was made to perform. If any part refuses its position, the entire equipment ceases to function.

A Blessing Becomes a Curse

The disastrous consequences of the violation of position are also seen in the power of death. Death is a constant companion for each of us. It is also the most unique motivator I have ever known. You can either fear death—negative motivation—or you can see it as an asset—positive motivation. It doesn't matter which path you take, you will always meet it at the end of the road. God wants you to learn about death so you can use it as a positive motivation and begin living.

Death has an assignment. This is true because God is a God of purpose who creates everything with a purpose. Nothing exists that was not created by God. Because death exists, it must have a purpose. The key, then, to understanding death is to discover its purpose.

Death has an assignment.

Death Defined

There are two definitions of death. First, death is "the extinction of vital functions to the point where they cannot be renewed." This definition applies to the lower order of life. For man, death is either "the separation of the soul and the spirit from the physical body" or "the separation of man, as an entire entity—body, soul and spirit—from God, his Creator."

The Scriptures tell us that death is the penalty of sin (Romans 5:12). We know, however, that Adam lived many years after he was driven from the garden and the tree of life (Genesis 5:5). Death, from God's perspective, must thus be the separation of man from Himself. He isn't so concerned with the length of your years as the state of your relationship with Him. It would seem, then, that the problem is not death, but the effect of sin on death.

The Servant Becomes the Master

Through sin, death began to do something that it was not supposed to do. It began to stop man's life. What God intended to be a blessing became a curse through man's disobedience. *Sin made death go in reverse. Instead of minis-tering dying, it is causing killing.*

Killing is death before the completion of purpose. Dying is death after purpose has been fulfilled. Death before the completion of purpose is murder because it stops you from doing all you came to the earth to do. This was not death's original purpose.

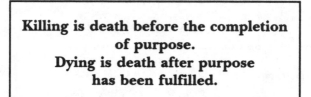

**Killing is death before the completion
of purpose.
Dying is death after purpose
has been fulfilled.**

God designed death to *produce* life, not *stop* it. *When sin entered the picture, death lost its purpose. It ceased serving your life and began to rule it.* Jesus came to get rid of sin and to deal with the one who is the source of sin.

Sin is everything that separates us from God. It is not so much what we do or do not do, as it is the attitudes of our hearts and our internal rebellion against the will of God. Thus, a person can be morally impressive but still be a sinner.

Sin caused death to go crazy. Consequently, death is now out of position. No longer the termination of an appoint-ment or the fulfillment of time as God designed it to be, death has become a power that thwarts God's purposes for individual people by claiming their lives before they com-plete, or even find, their purpose.

Death, when it assumes the role of a servant, is really a graduation from this phase of life to the next. It frees us from time and propels us into eternity. The death we now know rules instead of serving. Because it is out of postion, death has a sting, a power and a victory that were not part of God's plan and purpose.

If your life is terminated before you discover and fulfill your purpose, you are killed. However, if you know your purpose and complete it, you simply die. Everyone who completes his purpose dies with peace and confidence. Paul, the apostle, at his death, confidently stated,

> **...I am already being poured out like a drink offering, and the time has come for my departure. I have fought the good fight, I have finished the race, I have kept the faith** (2 Timothy 4:6-7).

This statement, like Jesus' declarations, "No one takes it [My life] from Me, I lay it down of My own accord" (John 10:18) and "It is finished" (John 19:30), indicates the peace that purpose gives in death.

Satan uses death for *termination*. God intended death for *transition*. The vast difference between the two is the result of death's change in position from *servant* to *ruler*. Although other violations of position may not have as severe a consequence as this, all deviations from God's intended purpose, and the resulting position, bring destruction and pain. They short-change all involved, causing either the loss or the deferment of achieving God's desired end. This is a high penalty for the temporary satisfaction that such infractions bring.

Satan uses death for *termination*.
God intended death for *transition*.

Purpose determines the right position. Any other position, no matter how good, is the wrong position. Life is too valuable to waste in the pursuit of status. God's position for all creation is always the best.

❖ **PRINCIPLES** ❖

1. Everything has a purpose, which determines its status in relationship to everything else.

2. Purpose is given to fulfill both the corporate and the individual purpose.

3. You cannot fulfill your purpose if you are in the wrong position.

4. Violation of position always causes chaos and destruction.

5. Death has become a threat because it is out of position.

6. God designed death to produce life, not stop it.

CHAPTER SEVEN

Purpose
and
Vision

Purpose gives precision to life.

Whenever I go on a trip, my secretary hands me an itinerary of what lies ahead. It lists where I will go, who I will see, how long I will stay and where I will go after I leave that place. Much of the information in my itinerary deals with flight numbers, arrival and departure times, the time zone of the new location and the names of the town to which I am going, the hotel in which I will be staying and the church in which I will be speaking.

In many ways, that itinerary organizes my schedule like purpose organizes my life. The value of known purpose cannot be overestimated, for it is the foundation upon which man must build his life. Life with purpose is precise and directed. It allows you to wake up in the morning confident that you know what you are supposed to do with the day. Life without purpose is depressing. Much needless energy is expended and much time is wasted as you move from one activity to another, busy but not focused. Purpose has this organizing value because it provides a vision, which motivates a plan of action to meet specific goals.

> **Life with purpose is precise and directed.**
> **Life without purpose is depressing.**

Purpose Provides Vision

The twenty-ninth chapter of the Book of Proverbs states: "Where there is no vision, the people perish..." (Proverbs 29:18a KJV) The New International Version translates this verse as follows: "Where there is no revelation, the people cast off restraint..." This is true because purpose provides a reason for existence. It encourages maximized performance toward an intended result. Or, to say it another way, purpose is destination—the end toward which something exists—and predestination—going back to start after seeing the outcome. When you know the desired end before you begin the journey, you are much more likely to stick with your task and stay on the prescribed path. *Apart from purpose, direction is lacking and nothing of importance happens.* Vision, then, is the direct result of purpose, providing the impetus to act on the direction set by purpose.

Defining Vision

The most common understanding of *vision* is "seeing," though that is not a completely accurate definition. *Vision* is more than seeing, for it moves beyond mere physical sight. Although the Greek word *opticia* (from which we get the words *optical* and *optician*, both of which deal with the eyes) is sometimes used in the New Testament to refer to vision, *hazons*, the most common Hebrew word for *vision*, means both "to see" and "coming into being." Thus, from a biblical perspective, *vision is the ability to see the end from the beginning*.

Webster defines vision as "the ability to perceive something not actually visible, as through mental acuteness or keen foresight." Thus, vision looks not at what is presently happening, but at what could or should be happening. It shows you something that has not yet taken place and registers it in your heart and mind. Vision is also "unusual discernment or insight" since it presents a picture of the unseen and convinces you that it will come to pass. Vision never stands alone. It always originates from a known purpose. Vision is a glimpse of purpose.

Vision Sets Goals, Which Motivate a Plan of Action

The primary value of purpose is the translation of vision derived from purpose into a plan of action. This occurs through the setting of specific goals. The presence of goals allows for both the development of a plan and the effective use of enegy as all efforts are put into the fulfillment of the purpose. Purpose maximizes energy and gives time meaning. Purpose protects you from being busy but not effective.

Purpose protects you from being busy but not effective.

Or to say it another way, purpose that is translated into a vision causes things to happen and people to act. This is true because purpose creates vision, vision produces goals, goals permit the development of a plan and a plan allows for an orderly journey.

Picture, for a moment, a train station with no tracks. Far in the distance walks a man, coming toward the station. Under his arm he carries wooden planks that he is throwing down before him, building the tracks to the station. The man's goal is to use planks to build a track to the station, which is his desired destination. His vision is the completed track, and his plan is the building of the track by throwing down the planks. Thus, the realization of his goal through the implementation of his plan will take him from his present position to the desired end, so that his vision of the completed track and his purpose of reaching the station are fulfilled.

Goals Are Steps Toward a Desired End

Goals are steps toward the attainment of a larger purpose. They create priorities, determine decisions, dictate companions and predict choices. Together they form the preferred flight plan to the desired destination. Let's examine how this process works by using the image of an airline ticket and the company that stands behind it.

> **Goals create priorities, determine decisions, dictate companions and predict choices.**

Long before I can book a flight or receive a ticket for a specific destination, some person had a purpose that gave birth to a vision that led to the setting of goals and the development of a plan. A purpose to provide safe air travel in the Western Hemisphere with quality service at affordable prices may have been prompted by too many business trips with extended layovers, canceled flights and delays caused by mechanical failures. In any case, the founder of an airline considers the possibility of starting a new airline and purposes to do so.

This purpose leads to a vision of planes servicing the entire Western Hemisphere, flying from Canada to Argentina, and everywhere in between. In his mind's eye, the soon-to-be airline executive sees his company's insignia on airplanes traveling throughout South America, Central America, the Caribbean, the United States and Canada. Fueled by his purpose and the accompanying vision, the originator of the vision calls in trusted friends and colleagues with whom he shares his thoughts. Others catch his vision and a new airline is founded for the stated purpose of providing safe, economical, quality air service to the Western Hemisphere.

Goals Encourage the Development of a Plan

Having a vision and receiving what you have envisioned are two very different things. Guided by their shared vision, the business man and his friends set goals for this corporation, determining when the flights will begin, which cities will be serviced by the initial service, what the desired profit margin will be and who will take primary responsibility for each area of operation. As these goals develop into a detailed plan, the person responsible for each facet of the business sets goals for their specific areas of operation and develops plans to meet these more specific goals.

Goals Dictates Companions

After the primary and secondary goals have been set and plans have been developed to meet each objective, the founding committee begins to seek those people who can help them to accomplish their purpose. Guided by their desire to offer quality service at affordable prices, they hire a research firm to survey the present airline market to see which flight routes are profitable and/or underserviced, and a financial consulting group to help them raise capital and develop an operating budget. Their aspiration to maintain safe, well-equipped airplanes prompts them to seek a highly-experienced airplane mechanic and a test pilot with an impeccable reputation. Together they will purchase the planes.

Finally, their ambition to provide quality service leads them to hire a personnel director who will initially oversee the development of a standard of service—after researching current airline standards—and later the hiring and management of company employees. Each of these decisions is based on the original purpose to provide safe, affordable, distinctive air service throughout the Western Hemisphere.

Goals Inform Decisions

As each of these people becomes part of the management team for the new corporation, they are charged with the responsibility of making their decisions based on the collective goals and purposes of the company. No one can pursue his own agenda if it detracts from the overall purpose of the plan. The financial consultant, for example, cannot require the mechanic to purchase an airplane that meets the budget guidelines but is not completely safe. Nor can the personnel director offer salaries and benefits beyond the means of the company. The choices each makes to fulfill his individual purpose must be influenced by the overall purpose of the company. No one aspect can be sacrificed for the others, or the company's reason for existence will be jeopardized. Purpose affects everyone's selections.

Goals Predict Choices

Purpose also serves as a guide for determining the best path to a predetermined end. Like a pilot's flight plan, it determines not only the final destination but also the best route on any given day to reach that destination. No pilot leaves the ground without a flight plan. Before he climbs into the cockpit of the plane, he carefully studies the maps, compasses and other instruments that can help him establish the safest, most direct course to reach the predetermined destination. Then he consults with air traffic control to determine where he needs to adjust his speed or altitude to allow for bad weather or other airplanes. Only after he has completed this task and received a stamped flight plan will he be permitted to guide the plane into the air.

> **Purpose serves as a guide for determining the best path to a predetermined end.**

Thus, when the pilot sits in the cockpit and presses the ignition to start the engines, he has with him both the end of the journey and the intended path to reach that end. Unlike a ticket holder who has only the vision of the final destination, the pilot knows both the final destination and the safest way to reach that airport. The choices he makes on the path to the final destination will always be guided by purpose and the goals related to purpose.

Goals Create Priorities

Even as goals directed by purpose predict choices, they also create priorities. If the new airline sets the first of September as the target date to begin service on the west coast of the United States, the research firm will not focus their attention on the east coast. That sphere of service will not be a priority. Likewise, if the goals include the objective of purchasing planes by the first of July, the financial consulting group will have to make the procurement of funds a priority so that this can happen. Purpose informs goals, which define priorities.

Purpose Provides a Measurement of Progress

As each target date on the master plan and the departmental plans passes, the executives are able to determine how well they are progressing toward their goal. If July passes into August, and the mechanic and the pilot have not yet procured any planes, the target date of September for beginning service on the west coast becomes doubtful. If, however, service on the west coast begins in mid-August, and additional planes have been purchased to begin service in the Caribbean, the organizing committee knows that they are farther toward fulfilling their purpose than they had expected to be at that point.

Without goals guided by purpose and the resulting vision, they would know that they are making progress, but they wouldn't have any idea whether that progress matches their plans for that specified time. The value of these goal-informed evaluations cannot be overemphasized because life without specific, measurable objectives is vague and haphazard.

> **Life without specific, measurable objectives is vague and haphazard.**

Obviously the above description of the process of beginning a new airline is very simplistic, but I think it provides an understanding of the value of known purpose. Known purpose enhances all of life, enabling a decisive, intentional perspective. This precise, deliberate perspective was visible in Jesus' life.

God's Timeless Plan

God is the source of all purpose. His plan to save mankind was the guiding purpose behind Jesus' coming to earth and all that He did and said while He was here. This purpose dictated His companions, predicted His choices, created priorities in His life, determined His decisions and provided a measure for progress.

Jesus made choices that fulfilled His destined purpose.

Throughout His life, Jesus was guided by the Father's predetermined will. In His baptism, He formally began to walk in that way by choosing to be baptized to "fulfill all righteousness." He who was sinless certainly did not need to be baptized for the remissions of sins, but Jesus was careful to do all that God had laid out for Him:

> Then Jesus came from Galilee to the Jordan to be baptized by John. But John tried to deter Him, saying, "I need to be baptized by You, and do You come to me?" Jesus replied, "Let it be so now; it is proper for us to do this to *fulfill* all righteousness" (Matthew 3:13-15).

His purpose predicted His choices. Again and again, the Scriptures record that Jesus acted in a certain manner to *fulfill* what God had predestined:

> When Jesus heard that John had been put in prison, He returned to Galilee. Leaving Nazareth, He went and lived in Capernaum, which was by the lake in the area of Zebulun and Naphtali—to *fulfill* what was said through the prophet Isaiah... From that time on Jesus began to preach, "Repent, for the kingdom of heaven is near" (Matthew 4:12-14,17).

> Do not think I have come to abolish the Law or the Prophets; I have not come to abolish them but to *fulfill* them (Matthew 5:17).

> ...the Pharisees went out and plotted how they might kill Jesus. Aware of this, Jesus withdrew from that place. Many followed Him, and He healed all their sick, warning them not to tell who He was. This was to *fulfill* what was spoken through the prophet Isaiah... (Matthew 12:14-17)

Jesus made decisions based on His purpose.

After His baptism, the Spirit of God led Jesus into the wilderness. As He fasted there for forty days and nights, Jesus came face to face with the reality of His purpose. He needed to set the reason for which He had been sent into the world firmly in His heart and mind so that He would not be deterred from fulfilling all that God have given Him to do. As He communed with the Spirit, satan came to Him with three challenges:

> The tempter came to Him and said, "If you are the Son of God, tell these stones to become bread." ... Then the devil took Him to the holy city and had Him stand on the highest point of the temple. "If you are the Son of God," he said, "throw yourself down." ... Again, the devil took Him to a very high mountain and showed Him all the kingdoms of the world and their splendor. "All this I will give you," he said, "if you will bow down and worship me" (Matthew 4:3,5-6a,8-9).

These challenges thrust at the heart of Jesus' person and message. Had He given into even one of the tempter's demands, He would have forfeited His purpose, for only One who was without sin could offer Himself as the ultimate sacrifice for mankind. Each time satan tempted Him, Jesus responded to satan's taunts by repeating the Word of the Lord. Because He was secure in His relationship with the Father, He could be committed to the Father's purpose for His life. At any time He could have used His divine powers, but Jesus chose to follow the path set before Him so that, through Him, you and I might discover our purpose.

Jesus' purpose influenced who He spent time with.

The value of purpose in Jesus' life is also seen in the people whose lives He touched. He came not just for the wealthy and the prestigious, though He certainly loved them, but He came also for the outcasts of society. Jesus' compassion for these "sinners" was particularly evident in the parables of the lost sheep, the lost coin and the lost son (Luke 15:1-32).

Jesus' desire to fulfill His purpose is also seen in the story of a tax collector named Zacchaeus. Tax collectors were hated by the Jews because these collectors worked for the Romans against their own people and often took more than the required taxes. They were also avoided by the Romans—except for the business of obtaining the required taxes—because they were Jews. This left tax collectors outside much of society. Yet it was to the home of Zacchaeus that Jesus went for dinner one night.

> **When Jesus reached the spot** [where Zacchaeus was watching from a tree], **He looked up and said to him, "Zacchaeus, come down immediately. I must stay at your house today." So he came down at once and welcomed Him gladly.**
>
> **All the people saw this and began to mutter, "He has gone to be the guest of a 'sinner.'" But Zacchaeus stood up and said to the Lord, "Look, Lord! Here and now I give half of my possessions to the poor, and if I have cheated anybody out of anything, I will pay back four times the amount." Jesus said to him, "Today salvation has come to this house... For the Son of Man came to seek and to save what was lost"** (Luke 19:5-10).

Jesus allowed His purpose to determine His priorities.

As the time for the fulfillment of His purpose drew near, Jesus began to speak of His coming death. His followers were upset. They could not believe what they heard. This was not the Messiah's destiny. Even Peter, one of Jesus' most intimate friends, could not comprehend a suffering Messiah:

> [Jesus] **then began to teach** [His disciples] **that the Son of Man must suffer many things and be rejected by the elders, the chief priests and teachers of the law, and that**

**He must be killed and after three days rise again. He
spoke plainly about this, and Peter took Him aside and
began to rebuke Him. But when Jesus turned and looked
at His disciples, He rebuked Peter. "Get behind Me,
satan!" He said. "You do not have in mind the things of
God, but the things of men"** (Mark 8:31-33).

How awful for Peter. Instead of taking his advice, Jesus
was rebuking him in front of the other disciples. But Jesus
could not allow Peter to stand between Him and the cross.
His purpose could not be served by Peter's desires. Whether
His friends went with Him or not, Jesus was determined to
stay on course. Even as He wrestled in the garden of Geth-
semane with the suffering the fulfillment of His purpose
would require (Luke 22:39-46), Jesus resolved not to avoid
anything God had predestined for His time on earth. He
knew that the cross was a priority that overrode even the
considerations of friendship, because death and resurrection were God's plan for His life.

*Jesus remained true to His purpose until He completed
God's plans.*

Purpose is a driving force. Against the greatest of odds,
it propels those who are committed to God's plans through
the worst of experiences. Betrayed, denied, beaten, crucified, Jesus remained true to His destiny. He trusted the
Father with His life (Luke 23:46) and yielded completely to
His God-ordained destination. As the agony of hanging on
the cross came to an end, "Jesus said, 'It is finished.' With
that, He bowed His head and gave up His spirit" (John
19:30).

**Purpose propels those who are committed to
God's plans through the worst of experiences.**

Jesus did what God sent Him to do. The barrier between God and man was broken forever and the curtain in the temple that separated God from His people was "torn in two from top to bottom" (Mark 15:38). Sin can no longer stand firmly between God and His children because "everyone who calls on the name of the Lord will be saved" (Acts 2:21). To all who receive Christ Jesus, "to those who believe in His name, He [gives] the right to become children of God—children born not of natural descent, nor of human decision or a husband's will, but born of God" (John 1:12-13).

Purpose, the Ultimate Pursuit

Purpose is the most valuable treasure you can find because it takes you beyond temptations, misunderstandings, the unfaithfulness of family and friends and even death itself. Thus, the passion for knowing and fulfilling purpose that was evident throughout Jesus' life must also be found in your life. Without that commitment to God's vision and the submission to God that allows Him to empower all that you do and say, you will forfeit your reason for being.

Choose now to make the fulfillment of purpose the passion of your life. Then set some goals to help you measure your progress. Finally, remain open to God's leading and direction as you follow His plans.

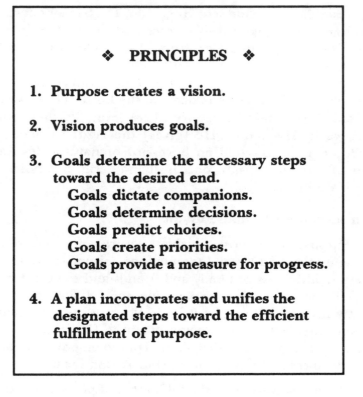

❖ **PRINCIPLES** ❖

1. Purpose creates a vision.

2. Vision produces goals.

3. Goals determine the necessary steps
   toward the desired end.
   Goals dictate companions.
   Goals determine decisions.
   Goals predict choices.
   Goals create priorities.
   Goals provide a measure for progress.

4. A plan incorporates and unifies the
   designated steps toward the efficient
   fulfillment of purpose.

CHAPTER EIGHT

The Benefits
of
Purpose

Without purpose, life is subjective.

Go with me in your imagination to a marina where large yachts come and go. As we arrive, you see a man standing on the wharf looking out to the sea. Youngsters surround him, fighting among themselves and periodically complaining that they are hungry. After a few minutes the man looks at his watch, then resumes looking beyond the harbor to the open sea. Ten or fifteen minutes pass and the children become more insistent in their demands to go home to supper. Finally, in the distance, a boat becomes a mere speck on the horizon.

As you watch the boat, it becomes evident that it is a white yacht with a large red flag on the stern. By now the man is smiling. He too has seen the boat with the red flag. As the sound of the boat becomes more audible and the name on the side visible, the man turns to the children in excitement. "She's coming. Mommy's coming!"

At that the children look at the man in surprise, for they did not know that they had been waiting for Mommy.

Immediately, they too begin to cheer and to shout to the people in the boat. As a slender woman emerges from the lower deck and climbs onto the wharf, she is swept into the corporate embrace of the joyous man and the clamoring children. The wait has ended and purpose has been fulfilled.

This word picture illustrates some of the benefits of known purpose. They are advantages that bless those who choose to find and obey God's predetermined will for their lives.

Confidence

First, purpose gives confidence. It assures us that what we are doing is the right thing. Thus, even though the object of the man's wait was not visible when he arrived at the wharf, he obviously expected his reason for being there to be fulfilled, for he waited until the yacht pulled into the harbor and his wife greeted him before he turned to go.

This same confidence due to an understanding of purpose was seen in the life of Jesus. The Gospel of Matthew tells a story in which Jesus healed a man who was blind and mute because he had a demon. When the religious leaders saw that Jesus had the power to cast out demons, they accused Him of receiving His power from Beelzebul, the chief of demons.

Jesus, unperturbed by their charges, used the image of a country or a family fighting within itself to show the falsehood of their allegations.

> **Any country that divides itself into groups which fight each other will not last very long. ... You say that I drive out demons because Beelzebul gives Me the power to do so. Well, then, who gives your followers the power to drive them out? What your own followers do proves that you are wrong! No, it is not Beelzebul, but God's Spirit,**

who gives Me the power to drive out demons, which proves that the Kingdom of God has already come upon you (Matthew 12:25,27-28 GN).

Confident in His God-given purpose, Jesus insisted that His power came from God, not satan. This same confidence in the power of the Holy Spirit in His life was visible when Jesus addressed the congregation in the synagogue at Nazareth.

The Spirit of the Lord is on Me, because He has anointed Me to preach good news to the poor. He has sent Me to proclaim freedom for the prisoners and recovery of sight for the blind, to release the oppressed, to proclaim the year of the Lord's favor. ... Today this scripture is fulfilled in your hearing (Luke 4:18-19,21).

Talk about confidence. By applying the words of the prophet Isaiah to Himself, Jesus boldly proclaimed that He was the Messiah. Oh, He didn't actually say that, but His listeners certainly would have made the connection. Knowledge of purpose gave Jesus the confidence to pursue His God-given tasks.

The same confidence is available to us. When we know what God intends for our lives, we can get on with it, assured that our work is not in vain. The Scriptures state that God's purpose will prevail (Proverbs 19:21), His purpose will stand (Isaiah 14:24; 46:10), and all His purposes are established forever (Psalm 33:11). In essence, when you discover God's purpose for your life, you can be confident and persuaded that you will succeed. This confidence will also inspire the trust of others. Purpose is the key to confidence.

When you discover God's purpose for your life, you can be confident and persuaded that you will succeed.

Protection

Second, purpose provides protection. In some ways this benefit of purpose is an extension of the first, because purpose gives the confidence that nothing can harm us until our purpose is finished. This includes not only the physical mishaps that might occur, but also the fear, worry and distractions with which the adversary may attempt to deter us from completing our purpose.

Thus, in the word picture with which we began the chapter, the purpose of meeting his wife protected the man from the distraction of the children that surrounded him. Had he been unsure which night the yatch was to arrive, he might have given in to the children's insistence that he leave the wharf and take them home to supper.

This protection occasioned by purpose is also visible in the life of Jesus. One day, Jesus and His disciples were crossing the Sea of Galilee when a storm arose that threatened to sink the boat. Jesus was asleep.

> **The disciples went and woke Him, saying, "Master, Master, we're going to drown!" He got up and rebuked the wind and the raging waters; the storm subsided, and all was calm. "Where is your faith?" He asked His disciples (Luke 8:24-25).**

Jesus couldn't die by drowning in a storm. That was not His destiny. His Father had sent Him to die on a cross for the salvation of mankind. No mere storm was going to interfere with that purpose. Therefore, He was protected from death by stoning and drowning because of the purpose of the cross. Purpose is your defense against premature death.

Purpose is your defense against premature death.

The same protection is available to all who know their God-given purpose, because God's purposes always prevail. Once God tells you His purpose for your life, relax. He's already told your predestination, so no matter how much pressure comes or how many problems threaten you, they cannot overcome you. When you know and live within God's will for your life, you are invincible until your purpose here is finished. Purpose doesn't make life easy. It makes it possible.

> **Purpose doesn't make life easy.**
> **It makes it possible.**

Perseverance

Third, purpose empowers perseverance. For the man on the wharf, purpose kept him standing, looking out to sea. As the minutes passed and there was neither the sound of a motor nor the sight of a boat on the horizon, purpose enabled him to wait for the desired end. He was not deterred from physically seeing that which he had envisioned.

Perseverance in the face of a seemingly desperate and hopeless situation kept alive the dreams of a biblical character named Joseph. The favored son of Jacob, Joseph was hated by his brothers. This animosity increased when Joseph had a dream and shared it with his brothers.

"Listen to this dream I had: We were binding sheaves of grain out in the field when suddenly my sheaf rose and stood upright, while your sheaves gathered around mine and bowed down to it." His brothers said to him, "Do you intend to reign over us? Will you actually rule us?" (Genesis 37:6-8)

We observe here that Joseph was envisioning his purpose for life. As a teenager he discovered his purpose.

Joseph's brothers became even more jealous when he had a second dream that he told to them and to their father.

"Listen," he said, "I had another dream, and this time the sun and moon and eleven stars were bowing down to me" (Genesis 37:9).

Although Jacob rebuked his son, he remembered what Joseph had said.

One day when his brothers were grazing their father's sheep, Joseph went to see how they were doing. When they saw him coming, his brothers plotted to kill him. One brother, however, convinced the rest to throw him into a dry well there in the desert. When a band of traders came along, another brother suggested that they sell him into slavery. Thus, Joseph went to the land of Egypt as a slave.

In Egypt he was sold to the Egyptian captain of the guard, whose wife accused Joseph of improper behavior toward her because he would not allow himself to be seduced by her. That landed him in jail, where he was soon put in charge of everything that happened there.

Some time later two Egyptian officials from Pharoah's household were emprisoned with Joseph because they had displeased the king. Each had a dream that Joseph interpreted for them. What Joseph foretold came true, although the official who was released forgot all about Joseph.

Two years later, Pharoah also had a dream. None of his magicians or wise men could tell him what it meant. Then the official who had been in jail remembered Joseph and spoke of him to the Pharoah. Joseph was thus brought from prison to interpret Pharoah's dream.

When Joseph was able to tell Pharoah the meaning of his dream, Pharoah put Joseph in charge of the preparations for the drought that he had foreseen. Thus, many years after he had dreamed it, Joseph's dream came true. His brothers came to Egypt to buy food. Not recognizing him, they bowed down before him when they were ushered into his presence, for Joseph was governor of the land and the one who sold grain to its people. In time, Joseph revealed himself to his brothers and told them that God had sent him ahead of them to Egypt to spare their lives and that of their father and their families. So, many years after God revealed His purpose to Joseph, the dream was fulfilled (Genesis 37; 39-46:7).

Many of us would have been very discouraged by the events in Joseph's life. But the memory of his dreams strengthened Joseph throughout the humiliation of being sold as a slave and the injustice of being imprisoned. His God-given purpose enabled him to use the opportunities that were before him and to cling to the vision he had received.

The same is possible whenever a person finds and acts on his destiny. Though the obstacles may be many and hard, purpose will ultimately triumph. Very often these hardships are part of the journey toward the fulfillment of purpose because they provide necessary experiences for the task ahead. Purpose, when it is seen and believed, can motivate us to keep on keeping on, no matter what.

> **Purpose will ultimately triumph.**

If you are convinced that what you are doing is God's purpose and will for your life, then no prison, pit or Pharoah can stop you. Stand firm in the face of adversity and persevere with a passion for your purpose.

Objectivity

Fourth, purpose introduces and maintains objectivity. It permits a view of life that looks beyond the apparent surroundings and the obvious pitfalls. Undaunted by the other boats that must have entered and departed from the harbor that day, the man on the wharf expected more than he saw. This hopeful attitude that looks beyond the evident problems in a situation is also observable in the life of the prophet Elisha.

> **Purpose permits a view of life that looks beyond the apparent surroundings and the obvious pitfalls.**

When the countries of Syria and Israel were at war and the king of Syria had set up camp in a certain place, Elisha warned the king of Israel not to go there, for he would be ambushed. After this happened several times, the king of Syria called his officers together and asked them who was on the enemy's side. One of them told the king that the prophet Elisha was telling the king of Israel where the Syrians set up camp. So the king ordered his men to find Elisha, so he could be captured.

When the report came to the king that Elisha was in a certain city, the king sent a large force of horses and chariots to surround the city by night. When Elisha's servant saw the armies surrounding the city the next morning, he expressed his fear to Elisha.

"Don't be afraid," the prophet answered. "Those who are with us are more than those who are with them." And Elisha prayed, "O Lord, open his eyes so he may see." Then the Lord opened the servant's eyes, and he

looked and saw the hills full of horses and chariots of fire all around Elisha (2 Kings 6:16-17).

Although Elisha's servant became fearful at the sight of the surrounding armies, Elisha saw something that his servant could not. That preserved him from fear and gave him an objective view of the entire situation. Elisha also knew that it was not yet time for him to die. No one was going to kill him before the Lord had gotten everything from him that He had purposed. Therefore, Elisha looked beyond the physical realm with the eyes of faith and cooperated with the Lord's plans, and the enemy became helpless in his hands.

The same is true in your life. When you are within God's purposes, your enemies are powerless to move you until God allows you to be moved. What you see in the natural is not all there is. God works for those who trust Him completely and expectantly. In essence, purpose protects you from being distracted by other people's assignments, good activities, unrelated works and company. Purpose keeps you focused.

> **Purpose keeps you focused.**

Contentment

Fifth, purpose sustains contentment. It supports a tranquility that refuses to be ruffled by the changing circumstances and states that pass through our lives. This peace that reaches beyond turmoil was evident in the watchful presence of the man on the wharf. He refused to allow either the quarreling children or the delay of the yatch to change his course.

This calm reliance upon a determined purpose is also evident in the life of the apostle Paul.

...I have learned to be content whatever the circumstances. I know what it is to be in need, and I know what it is to have plenty. I have learned the secret of being content in any and every situation, whether well fed or hungry, whether living in plenty or in want. I can do everything through Him who gives me strength (Philippians 4:11-13).

It was also Paul who confidently said: "He who began a good work in you will carry it on to completion..." (Philippians 1:6)

This testimony of calm assurance reveals the attitude of a man of purpose. This was not a man whose path was smooth, for Paul endured hardships that would throw many of us into despair. But Paul knew what God had ordained for his life. The obstacles that cropped up along the way could not deter him from completing all that God had given him to do, because his sufficiency lay in the Lord.

Purpose thus enabled Paul to cope with a myriad of hardships and blessings because of his contentment in the all-encompassing care of God. He recognized the inner peace he enjoyed as the gift of the God who enabled him to meet all life's circumstances with the same trusting perspective. He learned not to sweat the little things as long as the overall picture furthered God's will and plan.

This unwavering journey toward a predestined end is possible for all who find and pursue God's purpose for their lives. Purpose both sets a course after determining the end and encourages the traveler along the way. This gift of contentment is a primary benefit of purpose, for it lifts us above the everyday disappointments and trials that would hinder our progress toward the desired end. If you know that what you are doing is God's purpose for your life, relax, because He is the Author and Finisher of your life and destiny.

> **Purpose both sets a course after determining the end and encourages the traveler along the way.**

Joy

Sixth, purpose creates joy. It occasions the spontaneous affirmations that both precede and follow the successful completion of a desired end. The joy of both the husband and his children knew no bounds as the moment for which they had waited drew near. The surprise and delight of the children, who had not known the purpose for the sojourn on the wharf, particularly reveals the joy of purpose as it motivated them to forget their hunger and whining in the more delightful prospect of reaching that for which they had waited.

The New Testament shows that life illuminated by purpose can erupt into joy even in the worst of circumstances. Paul and Silas had been beaten and thrown into jail for healing "a slave girl who had a spirit by which she predicted the future" (Acts 16:16). Her angry owners, seeing the end of the fortunes the girl had brought them, seized Paul and Silas and charged them with creating an uproar in the city by promoting customs that were unlawful for Romans to follow. Now, with bleeding backs and feet secured in stocks, Paul and Silas were imprisoned in an inner cell.

"About midnight Paul and Silas were praying and singing hymns to God, and the other prisoners were listening to them" (Acts 16:25). As their thoughts turned to the One whose call on their lives had gotten them into this mess, the joy of knowing and serving the Lord overshadowed the desperateness of their physical situation. The sufficiency of their position within the will of God bubbled up within them and burst forth in song. Nothing, not even a dank, filthy Roman jail, could remove the satisfaction of living within the God-ordained purpose for their lives.

This joy in the midst of hell is the hallmark of those who have truly found God's purpose for their lives and have committed themselves to cooperating with it. They have learned that God will move the jail if necessary to permit them to accomplish everything that He has established for them. Such assurance produces a satisfaction that cannot be stolen. Purpose produces joy in those who are whole-heartedly committed to the way of the Lord.

> **Joy in the midst of hell is the hallmark of those who have truly found God's purpose for their lives.**

Intercession of the Holy Spirit

Finally, commitment to personal purpose brings the power of the Spirit's intercession on our behalf.

In the same way, the Spirit helps us in our weakness. We do not know what we ought to pray for, but the Spirit Himself intercedes for us with groans that words cannot express. And He who searches our hearts knows the mind of the Spirit, because the Spirit intercedes for the saints in accordance with God's will. And we know that in all things God works for the good of those who love Him, who have been called according to His purpose (Romans 8:26-28).

What power. Purpose has the capacity to lift you above your worries because the Spirit Himself is praying for you.

You're worrying and He's praying. He's praying for you to get what you need to fulfill God's purpose for your life. That's the key, because God works in the lives of those who are committed to His purposes.

If you entrust yourself completely to His will for your life, He promises you that He will take everything and use it for the accomplishment of His purpose. Nobody will move you until God says it's time to move. Your days are wrapped in His protecting love and concern.

Thus, the advantages that purpose brings are wrapped in this final and encompassing benefit. When the Spirit intercedes in your behalf and you are committed to the purposes of God, God is obligated to act for your good. That is the most wondrous blessing of knowing your purpose and living within it.

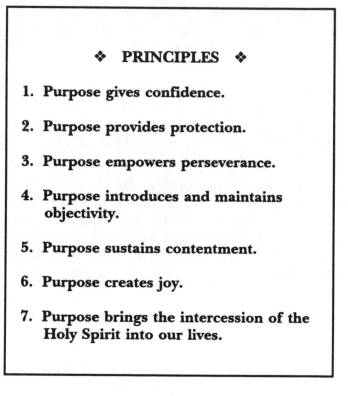

❖ **PRINCIPLES** ❖

1. **Purpose gives confidence.**

2. **Purpose provides protection.**

3. **Purpose empowers perseverance.**

4. **Purpose introduces and maintains objectivity.**

5. **Purpose sustains contentment.**

6. **Purpose creates joy.**

7. **Purpose brings the intercession of the Holy Spirit into our lives.**

CHAPTER NINE

The Source of Purpose

The source of purpose is the mind of the producer.

Have you ever noticed the delight of a child as he sees a butterfly or a bee up close for the first time? The joy and surprise first register in the eyes, soon to be followed by the expressiveness of words: "Look how pretty it is, Mommy. It looks so soft I want to touch him." Before long, however, the pleasure and wonder give way to a multitude of questions: "Why does the butterfly move its wings that way, Daddy, and why does it have those things on top of its head?" Or, "Why does the bee keep moving from one flower to another? Doesn't it get tired?" Thus, the joy of watching often gives way to the natural inquisitiveness of a child. The *what* is not enough. He wants to know *why*.

A Hopeless View of Life

Children are not alone in their desire to know why. The purpose or meaning of life, and all that it entails, is a frequent topic of everyday conversation, as well as a recurring theme in literature. William Shakespeare, an English playwright, reveals one outlook on life in his play *Macbeth*:

> **"Life's but a walking shadow, a poor player, that struts and frets his hour upon the stage, and then is heard no more; it is a tale told by an idiot, full of sound and fury, signifying nothing"** (*Oxford Dictionary of Quotations*, p. 461).

From this character's viewpoint, people are actors whose lives count for nothing. When the play's over, naught of value is left. Only emptiness and meaninglessness remain.

A similar perspective is found in the biblical book of Ecclesiastes.

> **"Meaningless! Meaningless! ... Utterly meaningless! Everything is meaningless." What does a man gain from all his labor at which he toils under the sun? ... There is no remembrance of men of old, and even those who are yet to come will not be remembered by those who follow. I have seen all the things that are done under the sun; all of them are meaningless, a chasing after the wind** (Ecclesiastes 1:2-3a,11,14).

The writer is laughing at man, showing the futility of his existence without God. Everything he does is empty. Indeed, life is so meaningless that nothing remains after his death. What a tragic understanding of life!

Nothing is more depressing than this hopeless view of life, a viewpoint shared by countless people. The question, "Why am I here?" beats in their brains, but they find no satisfactory answer. They walk through life doing everything that it requires of them, but none of it has meaning. Poor self-esteem, jealousy and a lack of consideration for others often characterize this life style, as each tries to find value by elevating themselves and belittling others.

This is not the way God planned for human beings to live. He intended that the purpose with which He created human beings and the world in which they live would define their lives. God wanted us to share His creative power, planning and designing and forming with purpose. But since we have lost touch with God the Creator through disobedience, we have also relinquished the awareness that life is based upon the basic principle of purpose. We no longer understand why God made us and what He intends for us to do during our years on earth. Without that understanding, we will never truly live or find personal fulfillment. It is essential, then, that we rediscover how to live with purpose by returning to the God who is the Author of purpose.

> **To discover how to live with purpose**
> **we must return to God,**
> **who is the Author of purpose.**

Purpose Is the Basis for Creation

The Scriptures teach us that God does everything in union with the purposes of His heart (Psalm 33:11; Jeremiah 23:20; 32:17-19). Nowhere is this more visible than in the creation story in Genesis.

Early in the creation record, the Bible tells us that God not only created things by speaking them into being but also gave each creation a purpose. Therefore, everything has a God-given purpose. The sky was created to separate the water above its expanse from the water beneath it (Genesis 1:6-8) and the land was given the purpose of producing vegetation and living creatures (Genesis 1:11,24). The lights God set in the sky were created to separate day from night, to serve as signs to marks seasons, days and years, and to give light to the earth (Genesis 1:14-15). God determined the purposes of mankind to include being fruitful and increasing in number, filling the earth and subduing it, and ruling over "the fish of the sea and the birds of the air and over every living creature that moves on the ground" (Genesis 1:28). God's purpose for man also required that he name all the birds and the animals (Genesis 2:19).

> **Everything has a God-given purpose.**

Thus we see that God, the Creator, is the source of purpose. Because purpose, by definition, is the end of a thing, not its beginning, the Book of Genesis—which is a story of beginnings—does not show us the full purposes of God. Its value for the study of purpose lies in its clear picture that God is the originator of purpose. Everything He created, including man, was made for a reason. It tells us *what* God did, but not *why* He did it.

Purpose Precedes Creation

Several years ago, my wife and I built a house. Of course the house was finished a long time before we built it—on paper, that is. Only after the architect had drawn a detailed plan on paper so we could picture how the constructed house would look did the carpenters start to build.

Everything in life is that way because that's the way God operates. He is a predestinator before He is a creator. He sets the end before He begins. In other words, God decides what He wants before He starts the process of getting it. He reveals the destination of a journey before He goes back to the beginning of the path that leads toward the destination. He sets the end before He starts working toward it, and predestines everything so that the purpose precedes the destination. Therefore, God had a purpose for creation and all that He created before He began speaking it into existence. If we want to discover this purpose of God behind the creation story—the intentions of His heart and mind—we must consider a larger picture than that presented in the Book of Genesis. Genesis is the beginning, not the destination.

> **God predestines everything so that the purpose precedes the destination.**

The Birth of God's Firstborn

To understand God's purposes behind the creation of the world, we must look at His first act of creation. The Book of Proverbs describes this first work of God's creative power:

> By wisdom the Lord laid the earth's foundation, by understanding He set the heavens in place; by His knowledge the deeps were divided, and the clouds let drop the dew.
>
> The Lord brought Me [Wisdom] forth as the first of His works, before His deeds of old; I was appointed from eternity, from the beginning, before the world began. When there were no oceans, I was given birth, when there were no springs abounding with water; before the mountains were settled in place, before the hills, I was given birth...
>
> I was the craftsman at His side. I was filled with delight day after day, rejoicing always in His presence, rejoicing in His whole world and delighting in mankind.
>
> For whoever finds Me finds life and receives favor from the Lord (Proverbs 3:19-20; 8:22-25,30-31,35).

The King James Version of the Bible translates verse 30 as follows: "I was daily His delight, rejoicing always before

Him." God delighted in the first of His works. He kept Wisdom at His side, sharing with Her both the work of creation and His delight in what He had made.

The Gospel of John gives this creative being at God's side another name:

> In the beginning was the Word, and the Word was with God, and the Word was God. He was with God in the beginning. Through Him all things were made; without Him nothing was made that has been made. In Him was life, and that life was the light of men. ... He was in the world, and though the world was made through Him, the world did not recognize Him. Yet to all who received Him, to those who believed in His name, He gave the right to become children of God... (John 1:1-4,10-12)

The Scriptures are clear that the Firstborn of God is none other than Christ, who took on human flesh in the person of Jesus. We see this in Paul's first letter to the Corinthian church, where he refers to Christ as the wisdom of God:

> Jews demand miraculous signs and Greeks look for wisdom, but we preach Christ crucified: a stumbling block to Jews and foolishness to Gentiles, but to those whom God has called, both Jews and Greeks, Christ the power of God and the wisdom of God. ... [He] has become for us wisdom from God—that is, our righteousness, holiness and redemption (1 Corinthians 1:22-24,30).

In Jesus, the firstborn Son of God—who in previous times had been known as the Wisdom of God and the Word—came to earth in human form. The delight God felt in the Wisdom is echoed in His pleasure in Jesus, as revealed at the time of Jesus' baptism.

> As Jesus was coming up out of the water, He saw heaven being torn open and the Spirit descending on Him like a dove. And a voice came from heaven: "You are My

Son, whom I love; with You I am well pleased" (Mark 1:10-11).

The first Son so blessed God that He wanted other sons and daughters in whom to delight. He wanted more children like His Firstborn. Thus, God determined to make human beings in the image of His first Son, who is the image of God Himself. That is God's motivation for creating us. Our purpose is to be sons and daughters of the Most High God in whom He can delight even as He delights in our older brother, Jesus Christ.

> **The first Son so blessed God that He wanted other sons and daughters in whom to delight.**

Paul's letter to the Ephesians tells us that God chose us long before the earth began, to fulfill His plans according to His purpose (Ephesians 1:4). God didn't accept us into His family as an afterthought. That has always been His purpose. Our adoption is part of His plan to bring everything "in heaven and on earth together under one head, even Christ" (Ephesians 1:10). We are the reason behind the creation story.

God got what He wanted. The first chapter of Genesis tells us that God made mankind "in His own image, in the image of God He created him; male and female He created them" (Genesis 1:27). His children, Adam and Eve, shared the likeness and image of Christ. But God wasn't satisfied with only two children like His firstborn Son. He wanted more children. Therefore, God blessed the man and the woman and said to them, "Be fruitful and increase in number..." (Genesis 1:28)

But the delight God knew in creating us did not last. With the entrance of sin into the world through the disobedience of Adam and Eve, God's children no longer acted

like Him. The Scriptures are filled with God's anguish over
His lost children.

> **The Lord looks down from heaven on the sons of men
> to see if there are any who understand, any who seek
> God. All have turned aside, they have together become
> corrupt; there is no one who does good, not even one
> (Psalm 14:2-3).**

> **They know nothing, they understand nothing. They
> walk about in darkness; all the foundations of the earth
> are shaken. I said, "You are 'gods'; you are all sons of
> the Most High." But you will die like mere men... (Psalm
> 82:5-7)**

> **He [God] said, "Surely they are My people, sons who
> will not be false to Me"; and so He became their Savior.
> In all their distress He too was distressed, and the angel
> of His presence saved them. ... Yet they rebelled and
> grieved His Holy Spirit... (Isaiah 63:8-10)**

> **When Israel was a child, I loved him, and out of Egypt
> I called My son. But the more I called Israel, the further
> they went from Me. ... How can I give you up, Ephraim?
> How can I hand you over, Israel? ... I will not carry out
> My fierce anger, nor will I turn and devastate Ephraim.
> For I am God, and not man—the Holy One among you.
> I will not come in wrath (Hosea 11:1-2,8-9).**

God Perseveres in His Purpose

God, who wanted His children to take after Him, refused to give up on them. He still yearned to be their Father
and to have them be His loving, faithful sons and daughters.
Although they had disappointed Him, He resolved to draw
them back to Himself, for His love would not be satisfied
until He again had sons and daughters to receive His love
and to love Him in return. Jesus is God's plan to restore His
children to His loving embrace. His purpose was to destroy

the works of the devil (1 John 3:8) and to save God's people from their sins (Matthew 1:21).

> **For God so loved the world that He gave His one and only Son, that whoever believes in Him shall not perish but have eternal life. For God did not send His Son into the world to condemn the world, but to save the world through Him (John 3:16-17).**

> **But God demonstrates His own love for us in this: While we were still sinners, Christ died for us (Romans 5:8).**

> **This is love: not that we loved God, but that He loved us and sent His Son as an atoning sacrifice for our sins (1 John 4:10).**

This desire of God to have children to love and to fellowship with is still the end toward which God works. He has created us to love Him and to be His children. That is the universal purpose of mankind, determined by the Creator before creation.

> **How great is the love the Father has lavished on us, that we should be called children of God! And that is what we are! ...what we will be has not been made known. But we know that when He appears, we shall be like Him, for we shall see Him as He is. Everyone who has this hope in Him purifies himself, just as He is pure (1 John 3:1-3).**

God Is Father

God, who creates everything with a purpose, has, among other expectations, given His sons and daughters the purpose of living in a loving relationship with Him that mirrors His union with His Son, Jesus Christ. The Gospels clearly reveal that Jesus knew God as His Father. He praised His Father (Matthew 11:25), did the work of His Father (John 5:36; 14:6-14), prayed to His Father (Matthew 26:39,42), asked His Father to forgive those who crucified Him (Luke 23:34), and committed His Spirit to His Father at His death (Luke 23:46). Continually, He spoke of God as "My Father" (Matthew 12:50; 18:35; Luke 22:29, to name a few).

The Scriptures are also clear that Jesus intended for us to think of God as our Father and ourselves as His children.

> But I tell you: Love your enemies and pray for those who persecute you, that you may be sons of *your Father* in heaven (Matthew 5:44-45).

> But when you pray, go into your room, close the door and pray to *your Father*, who is unseen. Then *your Father*, who sees what is done in secret, will reward you (Matthew 6:6).

> If you, then, though you are evil, know how to give good gifts to your children, how much more will *your Father* in heaven give good gifts to those who ask Him! (Matthew 7:11)

Perhaps the most notable evidence of this intention is the prayer Jesus taught His disciples to pray:

> This, then, is how you should pray: *"Our Father* in heaven..."* (Matthew 6:9)

Jesus came to reintroduce us to God the Father, not God the Creator. Through His life and teaching, He revealed the heart of God in a way that the Wisdom and the Word had not communicated. God's people knew Him as a judge and a consuming fire, but they had not learned that God is a father who wants to be close to His children. God sent us His Son so we could get the idea: "Tell them I'm Daddy. Reveal to them that they can call me 'Abba,' Daddy."

Jesus intended for us to think of God as our Father, and ourselves as His children.

God's desire has always been to be a father. His purpose for creating men and women, and His purpose for the people He created, is that we would know the close union with the Father that Jesus exhibited during His ministry on earth. God loves us like a father loves his children. He is always ready to care for us if we will but accept our place as His children and live in an obedient, dependent relationship that reflects the unity of the firstborn Son and His Father.

Destined to Be Like God

When Christ took on human form, He retained the likeness and image of God. Thus, He could say, "If you really knew Me, you would know My Father. ... I am in the Father and the Father is in Me" (John 14:7,11). He revealed the nature of God, a glory that He had shared with God before the world began.

> **Father, the time has come. Glorify Your Son, that Your Son may glorify You. ... I have brought You glory on earth by completing the work You gave Me to do. And now, Father, glorify Me in Your presence with the glory I had with You *before* the world began. I have revealed You to those whom You gave Me out of the world...** (John 17:1,4-6)

God's *glory* is His *true* nature in all its perfection. The glory of a flower is seen when it is at its prime. The glory of a sunset is visible when the colors are at their height. The glory of the sun is revealed at high noon, even as the glory of the moon is displayed in a full, harvest moon. Glory is always revealed at the point of perfection.

In the creation of mankind, God put His nature, image and likeness into us (Genesis 1:26). Then He said, "Go ahead. Express what I am," because He wanted His glory to fill the earth. The manifestation of God's nature is part of His purpose for our lives. This is possible because God was looking at Christ when He created mankind. He designed us, like Jesus, to be like Him. He has no desire for Christians, but for sons and daughters who share His interests, perspectives and visions. That was the nature of His fellowship with Adam and Eve in the garden.

> **God has no desire for Christians,**
> **but for sons and daughters who share**
> **His interests, perspectives and visions.**

Jesus came to earth to take us back to that garden relationship. His life showed us the fullness of God that we had been created to reveal. Because we are destined to show the world the same glory that Jesus' disciples beheld on the Mount of Transfiguration (Matthew 17:1-13), the Son of God and the Holy Spirit are now in the business of conforming God's sons and daughters into His likeness for the purpose of displaying His glory or His true nature.

Created to Reveal God's Character

The transformation that the Holy Spirit is executing in our lives includes the unveiling of the character of God within us that has been covered over by sin. Ephesians 1:4 tells us that God "chose us before the creation of the world to be holy and blameless in His sight." God doesn't want us to *develop* holiness, because He never intended that we would *not* be holy. Holiness is part of us because holiness is the nature of God in whose image and likeness we are created. Indeed, all the characteristics of God are present in our lives, whether we reveal them or not. In essence, the source of anything determines its nature, which establishes its natural qualities. The word *natural* is derived from the word *nature* and implies that which is of the essential

properties of an element. We came out from God. Therefore, we possess His natural qualities and nature.

> God doesn't want us to *develop* holiness,
> because He never intended that
> we would *not* be holy.

God's Spirit, whose fruit is "love, joy, peace, patience, kind-
ness, goodness, faithfulness, gentleness and self-control"
(Galatians 5:22-23), cannot be other than God is. When that
Spirit lives in us after our rebirth through faith in Jesus
Christ, those fruits are to be evident in our lives as well.
That's part of God's original intention for mankind. We,
who are sons and daughters of the Most High God, are to
bear a family resemblance to our Heavenly Father.

David, a Man of Purpose

The Scriptures are filled with the stories of men and
women who glimpsed God's purpose for their lives and bore
a family resemblance to God the Father. The faith chapter,
as the eleventh chapter of the Book of Hebrews is often
called, describes the actions and the attitudes of many who
accepted God's invitation to a purposeful, significant life
anchored in Him. Abraham, Noah, Jacob, Joseph. Moses,
Rahab, Joshua, Gideon. All discovered God's purpose for
their lives and remained faithful to what they had seen.

Perhaps no person in the Bible, however, better reveals
God's intended relationship with His children than King
David. *David was a man with a purpose.* From the time of
His anointing by the prophet Samuel to be king over Israel
to his death at an old age, David sought and obeyed the
plans and purposes of God. David learned early in his life

that God is not unapproachable. From his days in the pasture shepherding his father's sheep to his responsibilities in the palace, David depended on God for guidance, protection, inspiration and peace. His life was far from smooth and he knew the devastation of sin. But David always came to God with his triumphs and his failures.

The psalms of David are filled with both his jubilant worship in the Lord's presence and his tearful repentance with sorrow and mourning. David knew beyond the shadow of a doubt that his purpose had both come *from* God and been given *for* God. Such was his intimacy with God that he came to be known as a man after God's own heart (Acts 13:22).

This relationship between God and David is the desire of God for each of His children. He wants you to be a child after His heart. He doesn't want you to come chat with Him once a week in your Sunday best. His concern is for the purpose He has set for your life and the effect of that purpose on your daily living. He's much more concerned with the attitudes of your heart than the environment or the conditions in which you live.

God wants you to be a child after His heart.

God's purposes never fail (Psalm 33:11). He works in us "to will and to act according to His good purpose" (Philippians 2:13). The plans we make for our lives will not change His purposes (Proverbs 19:21). The primary question each of us must consider is whether we will discover and cooperate with the purposes of God or whether we will deny His fatherhood and withdraw from the fellowship and meaning that His presence gives our lives. *Knowing and following purpose is the key to a meaningful, healthy, joy-filled life.* God destined you to live *for* and *with* a purpose. He wants you to discover your individual and corporate purposes and to experience the rewards of finding them.

❖ PRINCIPLES ❖

1. God is the source of purpose.

2. God is a predestinator before He is a creator.

3. God chose us long before the earth began, to fulfill His plans according to His purposes.

4. Sin and disobedience destroyed our opportunity to live with God and to manifest His image and nature in the world.

5. God's purpose has not changed. He still wants children who act like Him.

6. We are destined to manifest God's glory to the world.

7. God's glory is His true nature in all its perfection.

8. God destined you to live *for* and *with* a purpose.

CHAPTER TEN

The Perils
of
Purpose

**Life without purpose is haphazard.
Purpose is the key to peace.**

As the hysterical woman carried the screaming child into the emergency room, the noisy room immediately became silent. All eyes turned toward the two who had stumbled through the door. For in her haste and great distress, the woman lost her balance and nearly fell. For a moment it seemed the child would surely tumble to the floor. Instantly, she caught herself and clutched at the slipping child. But not before an audible gasp passed through the room. Then their horror deepened as they saw the child's hands, arms and face. They were badly burned.

Later, after the child had been taken upstairs to a room in pediatrics, a nurse overheard the child and his mother talking.

"My arm hurts, Mommy," the boy whimpered. When his mother didn't reply immediately, he tore frantically at the bandages over his eyes and screamed in terror, "Mommy, where are you? I can't see you."

"I'm right here," replied the gentle, yet tearful, voice. "I know it's hard for you not to see me, but you mustn't pull at the bandages. Remember what the doctor told you."

"I know, Mommy, but everything hurts. And I was scared when you didn't answer me."

"I know, honey," came the soft reply.

As the mother watched her son, regret filled her eyes and tears streamed down her face. The unknown terrors ahead filled her heart and her mind. Then in the quiet the child asked, "Mommy, why are you crying?"

Surprised that the child—with his bandaged eyes and the sedating medicine the nurse had given him—could know that she was crying, the mother replied, with a catch in her voice, "I'm just sad that you're hurt, son. And I'm so sorry."

"I'm sorry too, Mommy. I didn't try to trip you."

"I know. But this is why I've warned you so many times to stay out of my way when I'm carrying hot things from the stove."

"I didn't know it would be *that* hot," the boy replied drowsily, as the medicine took effect.

"I'm sure you didn't," his mother answered, leaning back in the chair and preparing for her lonely night vigil.

The Peril of Ignorance

Ignorance! It is the most destructive force this world knows. It causes wars, poverty, fear and worry. It also destroys the lives of millions of people. Deadlier than satan or any force of evil, ignorance is the number one enemy of life.

According to Webster, ignorance is "the quality or condition of little knowledge, education or experience; unawareness." When ignorance is used to describe our understanding of purpose, it means that we have little knowledge, education or experience concerning the reason for our existence. We know neither the motive for God's creating us nor the end toward which our existence leads. We are unaware of His plans and purposes for our lives, and our existence becomes a trial and error game. Such ignorance is dangerous because it permits the possibility that we will live all our lives and never know why we lived.

> **Ignorance is dangerous because it permits the possibility that we will live all our lives and never know why we lived.**

Like the child who was not completely ignorant of the dangers of the stove, most of us are not completely ignorant of God's purposes. By now we know that God is the source of purpose; that purpose has a certain inherent, individual, multiple, interdependent, permanent, resilient and universal nature; that purpose is both governed by and revealed in a set of principles; that purpose has a priority over function, design, talents, potential, demand, provisions, promises, time and position; and that purpose is valuable, with a multiplication of benefits.

Knowing something and comprehending it, however, are often two very different experiences. Although we may know the facts and the correct words, it is very possible that we have not yet grasped the significance for our lives of what we know. Too often, knowledge without understanding gives a false sense of security that prevents us from giving our serious attention to the remaining steps in a process.

> **Knowledge without understanding gives a false sense of security.**

The journey of living with purpose requires a lifelong relationship with God our Creator. Because we are the creatures and He is the Creator, we must go to Him to discover all we were meant to be. Like the child who feared life without the closeness of Mommy, so too we need the closeness with God of knowing and being known.

The Value of Relationship

The word for *know* in Hebrew is *yadah*, which means "to go to bed with, to have a relationship with." It speaks of an intimacy that goes beyond casual acquaintance. "Adam knew Eve his wife" (Genesis 4:1 KJV).

Understanding and living with purpose requires insight beyond mere knowledge. It demands trust and loyalty that believes what it has seen and acts on that belief. God's principle of seedtime and harvest, for example, necessitates both the vision of the harvest and the planting of the seed. Thus, God blesses those who give freely, trusting in His sovereign care. Or consider God's promise that He will give us the needed words to witness for Him (Matthew 10:19). Knowing and believing the promise does nothing unless we act on it, trusting God to act in return.

Yet, even with this necessary element of trust, *knowing* in the biblical sense means more than believing and acting. It involves a oneness with God or another person that provides a true unity of purpose. Selfishness and jealousy vanish. Quarreling and reluctant cooperation become attitudes of the past. This unity of purpose between God's will and ours is the ultimate goal of God the Father.

> **Unity of purpose between God's will and ours is the ultimate goal of God the Father.**

Unity of Purpose

Purpose looks through the eyes of God, seeing the end, then moving back and starting toward what we have seen. It requires a passion for understanding and sharing God's vision that prompts us do things we would never attempt in our own strength. It obligates us to receive God's demands, however massive or insignificant they may appear, as the desires of a loving Father who is drawing from us all He placed within us for the good of the world.

Such living requires a depth of communion that allows the human spirit to hide itself in God, drawing from the Holy Spirit both the information and the resources to accomplish everything that has been purposed. It demands moving with, not against, the promptings of the Spirit, refusing to hang back when the Spirit says "go" or rush ahead when the Spirit says "wait." This life of purpose is not without its pitfalls, for ignorance is not the only peril of purpose.

The Peril of Despair

The most common peril of this intense knowing is the despair that creeps into our lives when the vision and the reality are far apart. As God's demands stretch our faith, we undoubtedly have periods when we stumble and falter, expending considerable energy on this business of living with purpose. The contrast between the glowing vision of what one day will be and the reality of our repeated ups and downs dampens enthusiasm. The prophet Elijah succumbed to this peril when he felt that he alone was responsible for ridding the land of false gods.

> Now Ahab told Jezebel everything Elijah had done and how he had killed all the prophets with the sword. So Jezebel sent a messenger to Elijah to say, "May the gods deal with me...if by this time tomorrow I do not make your life like that of one of them." Elijah was afraid and ran for his life. When he came to Beersheba in Judah, he left his servant there, while he himself went a day's journey into the desert. He came to a broom tree, sat down under it and prayed that he might die. "I've had enough, Lord," he said. "Take my life..." Then he lay down under the tree and fell asleep (1 Kings 19:1-5).

While he slept, an angel awoke him and told him to eat, "for the journey is too much for you." So Elijah ate and drank. Then he traveled forty days and nights to the mountain of God. There he met God.

> And the word of the Lord came to him: "What are you doing here, Elijah?" He replied, "I have been very zealous for the Lord God Almighty. The Israelites have rejected Your covenant, broken down Your altars, and put Your prophets to death with the sword. I am the only one left, and now they are trying to kill me too" (1 Kings 19:9-10).

When he obeyed the Lord's command to stand on the mountain in His presence, Elijah found that God was not in the wind or the earthquake or the fire. God spoke to him in a gentle whisper, telling him what to do next and assuring him that he was not alone.

> Go back the way you came, and go to the Desert of Damascus. When you get there, anoint Hazael king over Aram. Also anoint Jehu...king over Israel, and anoint

Elisha...to succeed you as prophet. ... Yet I reserve seven thousand in Israel—all whose knees have not bowed down to Baal and all whose mouths have not kissed him" (1 Kings 19:15-18).

So Elijah went from Mount Horeb and "threw his cloak on Elisha" (1 Kings 19:19). Strengthened by the Lord, Elijah moved on toward the completion of his purpose.

Despair, though a danger of known purpose, need not overcome us if we continue in relationship with the Lord, our God. Time in His presence strengthens us to remain faithful to the shared vision and purpose. On the other hand, trying to lift ourselves from the pit will not work.

The Peril of Idolatry

Prolonged desperation opens the door for idolatry, which is nothing more than replacing God with something else. Living with purpose always contains the temptation to focus more on the temporary struggles of the journey or the provisions for the journey than on the One who calls us to live and move and have our being in Him.

When the children of Israel saw that Moses delayed in returning from the mountain where he was talking with God, they sinned by molding and worshiping a golden calf (Exodus 32). Unwilling to wait for God to fulfill His purposes, they provided a god for themselves. Their impatience was a costly error. So angry was God with their impetuousness and unfaithfulness that He desired to wipe out the entire people and start again with Moses (Exodus 32:9-14; Deuteronomy 9:7-29). Even though the Lord relented from His intent to destroy the entire people, three thousand people were killed by the sword and the Lord sent a plague on those who remained.

Too often the impatience that undergirded the Israelites' disobedience is evident in the Church when we fail to wait for God's timetable. As our energies and resources become severely stretched trying to maintain a large building or extensive programs, we have nothing left for ministry. Such impetuousness always carries a price.

Oh, the resulting idolatry may not be as visible as the golden calf, but moving ahead of God's schedule always turns our sight from God to the process by which He works out His purposes. This deviation is not to be viewed lightly, for idolatry short-circuits our potential and detours God's work in and through us. It also removes us from the intimacy of vision and direction that God desires for His relationship with us, because God is a jealous God. He will not tolerate anything that replaces Him or removes our trust and affection from Him. We dare not become impatient and run ahead of God, for the peril of idolatry is a serious pitfall within the journey of finding and fulfilling the will of God.

> **God will not tolerate anything that replaces Him or removes our trust and affection from Him.**

The Peril of Arrogance

Limiting God is a peril that is related to but not synonymous with idolatry, because it also restricts God and wastes time, energy and resources. In essence, we bind God's hands because we presume that we know how and when He is going to work. This assumption leads to an arrogance that either interferes with the accomplishment of purpose or completely nullifies it by desensitizing us to God's direct instructions.

Although living in relationship with God does strengthen our understanding of His will, we will never completely see what He is trying to do or why, because His thoughts and ways are far beyond ours. King Saul had to learn the importance of obeying God's specific commands, whether or not they matched up with his expectations and desires.

When God anointed Saul to be king, He gave him some preservation clauses that would safeguard God's people and enable Saul to fulfill his responsibilities as their king. Through the prophet Samuel, God told Saul to attack the Amalekites and totally destroy everything that belonged to them. Nothing—men, women, children or infants; cattle, sheep, camels or donkeys—was to be spared (1 Samuel 15:3).

But Saul chose to disregard God's instructions. Saving "the best of the sheep and cattle, the fat calves and lambs" (1 Samuel 15:9), Saul resolved to offer these to God, for he was unwilling to completely destroy these many good things. Indifferent to the disobedience this involved, Saul told Samuel: "The Lord bless you! I have carried out the Lord's instructions" (1 Samuel 15:13).

God did not agree with Saul's assessment of the situation. He was grieved that He had made Saul king and He resolved to remove Saul from kingship because he had turned away from Him and had not carried out His instructions (1 Samuel 15:10-11).

Disobedience, either by disregarding God's instructions or by limiting how far we are willing to go with Him, is a pitfall that bears watching. We can never presume to totally know the heart and the mind of God, nor can we assume that we know better than God the nature and scope of His purposes. In other words, it is better to do what God tells you to do, than to do something nice for God. Disobedience is always wasteful and destructive because it reveals a pride and a presumptuousness that will ultimately destroy the person and forfeit the execution of purpose. The experience of King Saul is a grim reminder of the consequences of this peril.

> **It is better to do what God tells you to do, than to do something nice for God.**

The Peril of Criticism

Another peril of living purposefully is the tendency to criticize others when their vision and ours don't match up. Some of Jesus' disciples were guilty of this when they criticized a woman who anointed Jesus' feet with costly perfume (Mark 14:3-9). Because they did not know or understand what Jesus would soon experience, they could not fathom why such expensive oil was "wasted" instead of being sold at a profit that could have been given to the poor. Entangled in their efforts to do good, they misjudged the woman and her actions.

We dare not assume that others are wasting their lives if their actions and understandings are not the same as ours. By this world's standards, their lives may appear to be wasted, but kingdom values are the only standards that count. Doing good does not always equal doing right.

The Peril of Deception

Finally, the pursuit of purpose includes the danger of deception. This occurs when we either blame others for our shortcomings and inadequacies or rely upon them too heavily for direction and purpose. God's words through the prophet Hosea indicted both the people who were disobeying Him and the leaders who relished their wickedness. No one was exempt from the destruction and the rejection their corruption brought.

> **Let no man bring a charge, let no man accuse another, for your people are like those who bring charges against a priest. You stumble day and night, and the prophets stumble with you. ...My people are destroyed from lack of knowledge. Because you have rejected knowledge, I also reject you as My priests; because you have ignored the law of your God, I also will ignore your children. ... Like people, like priests. I will punish both of them for their ways and repay them for their deeds (Hosea 4:4-6,9).**

This rejection occurred not so much because of the unrighteous acts as the unfaithfulness to God that prompted those acts.

Faithfulness to God is a cornerstone to achieving purpose. Whenever we choose not to acknowledge Him and His foreordained desires for our lives, we open ourselves to the influence of the evil one. For satan knows what God intends for our lives and he will do anything to keep us from accomplishing it.

If you don't find your God-given purpose, satan will supply one for you, and he'll convince you that it's the right purpose. If, on the other hand, you know God's purpose and you're trying to live it out, satan will either push you too fast or he'll find ways to slow or detour your progress. Either temptation—embracing a false purpose or trying to use shortcuts and alternate routes to fulfill purpose—can only bring heartache and loss. Deception always occasions destruction.

If you don't find your God-given purpose, satan will supply one for you.

Beyond the Pitfalls

God needs you to accept and agree with His will for your life. He also needs you to commit yourself entirely into His keeping without taking your life back now and then when you question what He is doing or where He is going. Only then can you avoid the perils or pitfalls of known purpose that would sidetrack your pursuit of purpose. His plans and purposes will prevail no matter how long it takes Him to achieve them, but He will not override your resistance or excuse your disobedience. He cannot make you successful until you allow Him to undo and redo the results and the motives of your sinful inclinations, and to clarify and realign your distorted perceptions.

> **God needs you to accept and agree with His will for your life.**

The key to purposeful living is to take to heart the truth of Jesus' words—"Apart from Me you can do nothing" (John 15:5)—and to commit your life to pursuing purpose with a passion. Then you will know victory over the peril of ignorance and the pitfalls of known purpose, and you will experience the freedom to be a successful, happy, productive child of God.

❖ PRINCIPLES ❖

1. Knowing purpose and comprehending its impact on life may be very different experiences.

2. Understanding purpose and living within it requires insight beyond mere knowledge.

3. Purpose from God's perspective sees the end from the beginning.

4. Despair may enter our lives when the vision of our purpose and the reality of daily life don't match.

5. Prolonged despair opens the door for idolatry.

6. Arrogance that assumes we know how and when God is going to work interferes with the accomplishment of purpose.

7. Disobedience is always wasteful and destructive.

8. Doing good doesn't always equal doing right.

❖ NOTES ❖

CHAPTER ELEVEN

Purpose and Success

What good is it for a man to gain the whole world, and yet lose or forfeit his very self?
Luke 9:25

Everybody everywhere wants to be "successful," but only a very few people succeed. Millions are driven, possessed and preoccupied with this passion. They would sacrifice anything to be seen or accepted as "successful."

Success in today's world is usually defined by the superficial rewards glorified in the media: wealth, power, fame, luxury, prestige and recognition. Yet few of us have a firm idea what it takes to be or feel successful. It is easy to presume that a young corporate executive who rises to the top management position of a major corporation and earns nearly a million dollars a year is successful, but would the young man agree? That depends largely on the sacrifice he made to get to the top, the quality of his life outside work, and perhaps most significantly, his personal reason for pursuing his particular career.

If the young man has a positive sense of direction that encompasses his whole life, not just his professional career or bankbook, and if he understands why he wants what he wants, his accomplishments may give him genuine satisfaction, making him a success in his own eyes. If, however, he does not have this clarity of purpose, and especially if he has been struggling to live up to someone else's definition of success—be it that of a parent, a spouse or perhaps society in general—he is likely to reach the top of his professional ladder but wonder why he feels so dissatisfied and burned out.

In the end he may realize that his identity as an individual has been compromised by the forces pushing him to attain career stardom. He has become trapped by the pressure to get ahead, and his life is out of balance. There are millions like this young executive who are striving daily after a prize they despise, to accomplish a goal they personally hate.

We, as a society, have confused success with fulfillment, accomplishment with satisfaction, and achievement with peace. I believe it is essential for you and for me to look beyond the wonderful things material success can buy, to the heavy price it can exact. You must question why you are so driven to succeed and why you've made the choices and the sacrifices that have shaped your private and professional life thus far.

> **We have confused success with fulfillment, accomplishment with satisfaction, and achievement with peace.**

Can you recall the personal goals that motivated you before external success became your life's ambition? Do you remember the origins of your assumptions about success? After you've traced the development of your personal definition of success, you must consider what it means to be true to yourself.

Few of us ever stop to develop a personal and meaningful definition of success that allows us to thrive as well as strive. Instead, we absorb a composite of largely superficial illusions from the media, parental demands and peer pressure. *In essence, success in our culture requires becoming what everyone else tells you to be.* It is assumed, almost as an afterthought, that success by the world's standards will magically include happiness, but this formula leaves little room for genuine personal fulfillment.

Most people look at those who appear to be successful and think they would be fools to change their jobs or life styles, even if they hate what they are doing. Not surprisingly, life dominated day after day, year after year, and one step up the ladder after another by this quest for success becomes increasingly less satisfying and more anxious. Millions of people live at this critical point, trapped between external success and internal collapse. In simple terms, success is not as simple as we once thought.

Success Defined

What is success? By now it must be obvious that I am questioning the world's perception of success. Success has very little to do with what you accumulate, possess or achieve. It has even less to do with other people's opinions and their assessment of you and your accomplishments. *Success can only be defined by purpose and measured by obedience.* The following statements support this premise.

- Purpose is the original intent for the creation of a thing. It is the reason for its existence and the why behind something's existence. Purpose is the "assignment" that is produced by the intent of the creator or manufacturer.

- Completion of the intended assignment is the fulfill-ment of the reason for existence. Being true to the original intent is the essence of obedience and the measure of faithfulness.

- The satisfaction and pleasure of the manufacturer when the product fulfills his intended purpose is the measure of success.

- Success is the fulfillment and the completion of the original intent for the creation or the production of a product.

- Success is obedience to purpose.

- Success is not what you have done compared to what others have done, but what you have done compared to what you were supposed to do.

> **Success can only be defined by purpose and measured by obedience.**

The above statements show that success has more to do with *being* than *doing*. To be successful is to *finish the originally intended assignment according to the plan and the specifications of the creator*. Purpose is thus the key and the foundation of success. It is the only true source of fulfill-ment and the only accurate measurement of life. Therefore, success cannot be determined by the opinions of others about your actions, but by the satisfaction of the One who gave you the assignment.

You are not successful if everyone says you are. You are not successful if you have done what others expected you to do. You are not successful if you receive commendation and recognition from your peers or the accolades of the masses. *You are truly successful only if you have done what you were purposed to do.*

Purpose is doing not a *good thing,* but the *right thing.* As *"the best"* is the enemy of *"the good,"* so the enemy of *"the right thing"* is *"a good thing." It is dangerous to do a good thing at the expense of the right thing.* Yet, there are thousands of people, even in the Church, who are busy doing good things that God neither told them to do nor purposed for their lives. (Many ministers are wearing themselves out pursuing ministry goals, projects, programs and assignments that are not part of God's plans for them.) They have adopted another man's vision or purpose as their personal standards for competition and comparison. Trapped by the expectations of others, they live to please everyone except God.

> **Purpose is doing not a *good thing,*
> but the *right thing.***

Be careful not to confuse right with good, famous, big, easy, acceptable or popular. Your only responsibility is to respond to God's purpose for your life. Your only measure of success is to find your purpose for your life and do it! *Living with purpose is the difference between being busy and being effective.* Don't let the tragedy of faithfulness to the wrong thing waste your life. Refuse to allow activity without progress to dominate your existence. Purpose protects you from doing good at the expense of doing right.

Jesus is the perfect example and the ultimate display of an individual who knew and understood the nature of success. Because He knew His purpose, He was protected from the opinions of others and the distractions of doing good.

Many times He expressed His understanding of His purpose in words like, "for this cause came I into the world," or "for this reason was the Son of Man manifested." His awareness of His purpose not only protected Him from distracting activity, it also served as the reference point from which He made His decisions and measured His success. At the completion of His assignment He could declare, "It is finished." Until you are able to say these words with assurance, your life will never be fulfilled and you will live another person's life.

You Must Discover Your Purpose!

I know deep inside you there is a cry and an agreement that confirms the truth that you were born for a purpose. You can feel the desire to reach for something greater than just making a living. I know you are tired of the rat race, trying to keep up with everyone, attempting to live up to their expectations. You despise the job you go to every day, and the ministry has become a source of frustration. Not even the presence of the Holy Spirit fills the emptiness inside.

Perhaps, you have never made a spiritual commitment to your Creator through Jesus Christ, and you are living a life of frustration. Perhaps all your accomplishments and achievements have brought you more frustration and disillusionment than joy. Maybe you have succeeded in fooling everyone that you are a success by meeting their expectations, but deep inside you have failed to be true to your inner dreams. You have made everyone happy except you.

If this nightmarish existence describes your life, you have not yet discovered your purpose. I, therefore, urge you to make a quality decision today to submit your life to your Creator and Manufacturer. *Remember, nobody knows the purpose of a product except the one who made or created it.* You were created by God the Father, and only He knows the purpose for which He gave you birth. He knows His plans for your life and the reason He gave you breath. He wants you to be fulfilled.

He is not asking you to be religious, only to reestablish a relationship with Him that can give you the resources to move from emptiness to personal satisfaction. Only then can you resume your purpose in life and find the personal and corporate fulfillment you desire. If you wish to surrender your life to Him, I encourage you to pray the following from your heart:

Dear Father God,

Creator and Manufacturer of my life, I am aware that You have created me for a specific purpose and designed me to fulfill that intent. I am aware that we as men have fallen away from You by our disobedience and have thus lost a sense of our purpose in life. I am also aware that You sent Your Son, Jesus the Christ, to restore us to You so that we can once again discover our reason for being. I, therefore, ask You, in the name of Jesus, to cleanse my life and send the Holy Spirit into my heart right now to reveal to me Your purpose for my life. I also submit to Jesus as my Lord and personal Savior and commit myself to finishing the assignment You have for me.

In the name of Jesus I pray,
Amen.

If you have prayed this prayer, write to me at the following address and share your decision with me:

Bahamas Faith Ministries International
PO Box N9583
Nassau, Bahamas

May God bless and enrich your life as you begin the journey of discovering and completing your purpose.

❖ NOTES ❖

CHAPTER TWELVE

A Word
to the
Third World

Purpose allows you to be yourself.

Most of the world's people, in every nation, culture, socioeconomic condition and political situation, are enduring lives that are daily drudgery. Even in the highly developed, industrialized states where wealth and affluence are easily accessible, millions experience depression, despair, anxiety and emptiness. They have come to realize that possessions, fame, status and power can never be substituted for a personal sense of purpose and significance.

> **Possessions, fame, status and power
> can never be substituted for a
> personal sense of purpose and significance.**

This truth is especially important for those who live in nations known as Third World countries. Many undeveloped, underdeveloped and now developing countries were victims of oppression, subjugation and colonization.

They were raped of dignity, self-worth and a sense of well-being. Most do not have access to the material possessions that the industrialized cultures use as the standards of wealth and success. This further compounds the frustration and despair among these people.

As a result, many Third World people, including those in the United States, Canada, England and other industrialized states, believe that their personal fulfillment, success and happiness are determined by their achieving the standard of success and status established by their oppressor. This further results in a poor self-concept and a negative attitude toward themselves.

If you believe that others hold the key to your success and fulfillment, then you will live to please them and to fulfill their expectations. You will also rely on their affirmation, approval and acceptance to measure the value of your life. This is a great tragedy because *it places your self-worth at the mercy of the opinions of others.*

> **If you believe that others hold the key to your success and fulfillment, then you will live to please them and to fulfill their expectations.**

This standard of measuring success is the source of much Third World frustration as nations find it difficult to break the sophisticated patterns of colonization and oppression, and millions of individuals live in a cycle of aimlessness, depression and poverty. This striving to imitate the industrialized world's patterns for success also breeds distrust and causes in-fighting among members of the same ethnic and socioeconomic strata as each contends for advancement and the control of material resources that promise them the fulfillment of their desires. This success trap will not bring true fulfillment or freedom, but greater bondage.

True freedom and fulfillment are possible only as you discover and understand your personal purpose. When you come to the realization that each person in the world has been created and designed for a specific and unique purpose, and that no one can be substituted for another, you are freed from the jealousy and the envy that fuel your desperate attempts to gain recognition at the expense of others.

> **True freedom and fulfillment are possible only as you discover and understand your personal purpose.**

You must accept the fact that there is something you were born to do that no one else can do with your particular satisfaction or expertise. This assignment is God's purpose for your life. Because He promises that His purposes will prevail, you and your nation do not need to compromise or sacrifice your values, convictions, morals or standards to achieve this vision. Your purpose is His vision. Therefore, He will make the necessary provisions for you to accomplish that vision.

I, therefore, encourage you to *declare independence from the expectations and the opinions of others. Defy their standards of success and refuse to imprison your identity within the life style or the preferences of another.* Decide today to be yourself so you can maximize your potential and fulfill your purpose. Remember, your purpose is that dream, vision, deep desire or lifelong idea that you hunger to accomplish. Obey God and keep His commandments. Please Him and complete your assignment. Only then will you find true success, for *the fulfillment of purpose is God's measure of success.*

Exciting titles
by Dr. Myles Munroe

◣ UNDERSTANDING YOUR POTENTIAL
This is a motivating, provocative look at the awesome potential trapped within you, waiting to be realized. This book will cause you to be uncomfortable with your present state of accomplishment and dissatisfied with resting on your past success.
ISBN 1-56043-046-X

◣ RELEASING YOUR POTENTIAL
Here is a complete, integrated, principles-centered approach to releasing the awesome potential trapped within you. If you are frustrated by your dreams, ideas, and visions, this book will show you a step-by-step pathway to releasing your potential and igniting the wheels of purpose and productivity.
ISBN 1-56043-072-9

◣ MAXIMIZING YOUR POTENTIAL
Are you bored with your latest success? Maybe you're frustrated at the prospect of retirement. This book will refire your passion for living! Learn to maximize the God-given potential lying dormant inside you through the practical, integrated, and penetrating concepts shared in this book. Go for the max—die empty!
ISBN 1-56043-105-9

◣ SINGLE, MARRIED, SEPARATED & LIFE AFTER DIVORCE
Written by best-selling author Myles Munroe, this is one of the most important books you will ever read. It answers hard questions with compassion, biblical truth, and even a touch of humor. It, too, is rapidly becoming a best-seller.
ISBN 1-56043-094-X

◣ IN PURSUIT OF PURPOSE
Best-selling author Myles Munroe reveals here the key to personal fulfillment: purpose. We must pursue purpose because our fulfillment in life depends upon our becoming what we were born to be and do. *In Pursuit of Purpose* will guide you on that path to finding purpose.
ISBN 1-56043-103-2

◣ THE PURPOSE AND POWER OF PRAISE & WORSHIP
God's greatest desire and man's greatest need is for a Spirit-to-spirit relationship. God created an environment of His Presence in which man is to dwell and experience the fullness of this relationship. In this book, Dr. Munroe will help you discover this experience in your daily life. You are about to discover the awesome purpose and power of praise and worship.
ISBN 0-7684-2047-4

◣ THE PURPOSE AND POWER OF GOD'S GLORY
Everywhere we turn, we are surrounded by glory. There is glory in every tree and flower. There is the splendor in the rising and setting sun. Every living creature reflects its own glory. Man in his own way through his actions and character expresses an essence of glory. But the glory that we see in Creation is but the barest reflection of the greater glory of the Creator. Dr. Munroe surgically removes the religious rhetoric from this often-used word, replacing it with words that will draw you into the powerful presence of the Lord. *The Purpose and Power of God's Glory* not only introduces you to the power of the glory, but practically demonstrates how God longs to see His glory reflected through man.
ISBN 0-7684-2119-5

Available at your local Christian bookstore.

For more information and sample chapters, visit www.destinyimage.com

5B-3:135

Additional copies of this book and other
book titles from DESTINY IMAGE are
available at your local bookstore.

For a complete list of our titles,
visit us at www.destinyimage.com
Send a request for a catalog to:

Destiny Image® Publishers, Inc.

P.O. Box 310
Shippensburg, PA 17257-0310

*"Speaking to the Purposes of God for This
Generation and for the Generations to Come"*